AF881847

Stepparenting Without Guilt

"It was with great relief that I recently discovered Maurine Doerken's new book, *Stepparenting Without Guilt.* In a nation that has a 50% divorce rate, the breaking apart and subsequent rearranging of family units is a too-common occurrence, and it is the children of broken homes who must bear a large part of the wound. Ms. Doerken, a Marriage and Family Counselor, has experienced being the 'mom who isn't a mom' with her own stepdaughter and knows first-hand of what she speaks. I would suggest that *Stepparenting Without Guilt* be the first book on every couple's list who are dealing with the 'yours, mine, ours' syndrome."

—Cathleen Rountree, author of the series,
On Women Turning 30, 40, 50, 60, 70

"In *Stepparenting Without Guilt,* Maurine Doerken takes us gently but firmly by the hand through the shadows and opportunities inherent in stepfamily life. With her encouragement, we face the many emotional and logistical demons along the path of raising stepchildren. Her guidance is clear and practical. The book will serve a wide range of parents contemplating or already embroiled in the adventure of stepparenting."

—Jack Zimmerman: counselor, educator and author of
The Way of Council (in collaboration with Virginia Coyle)
and *Flesh and Spirit: The Mystery of Intimate Relationship*
(co-authored by Jaquelyn McCandless)

"An extremely helpful guide—not just for stepfamilies, but everyone trying to improve their family dynamics. *Stepparenting* is filled with practical suggestions, honest evaluations and profound insights into family life. A must-read."

—Ken Cloke, Center for Dispute Resolution, author of *Mediation: Revenge and the Magic of Forgiveness*

"Reading *Stepparenting Without Guilt,* I was surprised to learn that there are more Americans in stepfamilies today than there are in first families. The information in this book is crucial, not simply because both parents and stepparents want a loving family environment for their children and themselves, but because the tools and insights offered herein remove the inevitability of making many of the mistakes that result in long-term damage to family relationships. If I had read this book during my first and second marriages, I might not have endured some of the confrontations that spawned my own book. Maybe I'd still be in my first marriage."

—Matt Kramer, author of *Conversations Before a Marriage*

"Maurine Doerken has done the impossible—assuaged my guilt for not knowing how to solve all the problems relating to stepparenting. I judged myself for not being as organized as my son's stepmother, and for not knowing how to save my stepson who came to me with a drug addiction. These issues didn't grow slowly; they happened at once.

"Maurine's book, *Stepparenting Without Guilt,* clearly sets before us the 'things that can be done' through communication, patience, and love. She also keeps ever present the notion that sometimes, and for a long time, your best efforts may fail.

"I couldn't help thinking while reading this book that we have created situations requiring the wisdom of Solomon, the patience of Job, and the loving heart of God. If we can create peace in the stepfamily, perhaps there is hope for the world. This complex generation is indebted to Maurine Doerken for her insight and clarity with which this book abounds."

—Cynthia Waring, author of
Bodies Unbound, Transforming Lives Through Touch

Stepparenting Without Guilt

Maurine Doerken

Blue Dolphin Publishing

Published by Blue Dolphin Publishing, Inc.
P.O. Box 8, Nevada City, CA 95959
Orders: 1-800-643-0765
Web: www.bluedolphinpublishing.com

ISBN: 1-57733-054-4

Library of Congress Cataloging-in-Publication Data

Doerken, Maurine.
Stepparenting without guilt / Maurine Doerken.
p. cm.
Includes bibliographical references.
ISBN: 1-57733-054-4
1. Stepparents—United States. 2. Parenting—United States.
3. Parent and child—United States. I. Title.

HQ759.92 .D64 1999
306.874—dc21

99-055730

Cover design: Lito Castro

Printed in the United States of America

10 9 8 7 6 5 4 3 2 1

For Peter and our four children
and other families living in step

"Happily ever after was invented by someone
who did not have a stepchild."

Delia Ephron
Funny Sauce

Table of Contents

Acknowledgments

I WOULD LIKE TO THANK the following friends, colleagues, and relatives who have contributed their time and feedback to this book:

Anjani Arcemont, Alan Bloch, Bill and Sara Margaret Bollinger, David Gordon, Daphne Lee, Susan Malter, Aletheia Morden, Cathleen Rountree, and Jack Zimmerman.

In addition, I would like to thank my familiy members, Peter, Melissa, David, William, and especially Nikki (who now goes by her first name Alex) for living through this stepfamily experience with me and for their help and support in the realization of this manuscript.

Finally, special thanks to Charles Guyton Anderson, III, whose generosity has contributed to this project more than he will ever know.

Introduction

When I began working on *Stepparenting Without Guilt,* I wanted to understand why stepparenting, even more so than biological parenting, felt so daunting and challenging a task. It was (and is) my hope that sharing these difficulties and experiences will help facilitate the process of being a better stepparent for others.

I think one of the main issues that confronts most stepparents is being unprepared beforehand and caught off-guard by how different this type of family can feel and be. It also requires facing the possibility of many personal interactions that require unique tools and communication techniques. These complexities are of both a practical and an emotionally demanding nature: organizing schedules, negotiating visitation and custody rights, planning transportation, caring for the personal belongings of children going back and forth between homes (clothes, toys, notes, etc.)—and dealing at times with ambivalent and painful feelings: anger, jealousy, and hurt along with unresolved grief over the loss of the original family unit. Intact families do not have to address these same issues.

To that end, I have formulated a number of stepfamily "rules" throughout *Stepparenting Without Guilt* which address some of these differences. I want to stress here, however, that rules, especially in family life, step or otherwise, can never be etched in stone. One of the hallmarks of stepfamily living is being able to embrace diversity and learning how to negotiate in a proactive rather than reactive manner. More than anything else, it is my hope that these so-called "rules" will provide useful guidelines for positive dialogue among stepfamily members and foster smoother sailing on what at times can feel like turbulent seas.

With divorce statistics seemingly ever on the rise, the importance of sound stepparenting is as important an issue today as sound biological parenting, perhaps even more so. I am happy to say after nearly twenty years on the job that there *are* rewards to being a stepparent, and I am really quite glad about being able to write that. Yet, as with most achievements in life that are personally satisfying, they require work, patience, and commitment to being part of a family structure that is different from what many of us experienced while growing up.

Chapter One, "Stepfamily Ties and Tribulations," provides an overview of some of the issues facing stepfamilies, particularly the myths and negative stereotypes associated with the word "step." Chapters Two and Three, "Life after Divorce" and "Period of Adjustment," focus more specifically on legal and court issues, scheduling tactics, discipline, and managing the various behavioral responses (from more difficult to easier) between two household families.

Chapter Four, "A Mom Who Isn't a Mom," focuses on stepmotherhood as that is what I know best, but I also have included material relevant to fathers and stepfathers as well. Chapter Five, "The Emotional Minefields of Stepfamily Life," addresses some of the more painful emotional experiences of stepfamily life and is applicable to all members of an extended family regardless of role or gender: parent, stepparent, or stepchild.

Chapters Six and Seven, "Council and Communication" and "Relationship Saving Suggestions," offer techniques for dialogue and information on communication skills. I have also included what one might call my philosophical approach to stepfamily and family interaction. I have found it helps to have an overall framework from which to function over and above specific guidelines and rules. I am the first to admit, however, that when you are in the throes of stepfamily formation and adjustment it is easy to lose sight of this philosophical blueprint (if it has ever been in sight at all!).

This leads me to a final point:

The word "love" is so overused in our culture today and frequently misunderstood. I do believe, however, that the fountainhead or foundation for success in stepfamily life is just that: love—not as a feeling, for it is easy to say "I love you"—but rather as an *act,* something which is far more challenging. And while I do not believe a successful stepparent has to *feel* love for his or her stepchildren or for the former partner (or partners) of a new spouse, to *act* love is another matter. It is also a choice, a very important one at that.

As we are increasingly faced with more and more people, different cultural and political perspectives, alternative ways of doing and envisioning the world, I believe it is vital, if not imperative, that we learn how to honor and respect that which is different from us. I can think of no other training ground better suited to this than being in a stepfamily. To that end, I hope *Stepparenting Without Guilt* proves fruitful to others who are thinking of embracing or who have already embarked upon this family path.

Maurine Doerken
Santa Monica, California
January, 2000

Stepparenting
Without Guilt

CHAPTER ONE

Stepfamily Ties and Tribulations

RECENT STUDIES SHOW that the loss of a parent by death may actually be *less* devastating to young people than losing a parent through divorce.[1] There are a number of reasons for this, but I think my stepdaughter put it the most eloquently: a child is better able to understand the fact of biological death than the complex reasons why love and marriages fall apart. This does not mean children accept death easily, but often it is less confusing for them to deal with both emotionally and psychologically than trying to understand why their parents have left one another.

When a stepfamily later is created, this coming together of new relationships often exacerbates the previous sense of loss rather than assuaging it—as many of us who remarry have experienced. This is one of the reasons why looking at the experience of stepfamily life is so difficult. More often than not, individuals beginning a stepfamily are required to confront many painful issues at the onset, without much time for reflection. Children have to confront a parent who has gone away and is not always there; both young people and adults have to adjust to one another rapidly while still feeling like strangers; and a previous love that has failed and former family life must be relinquished forever. This makes the many issues of stepfamilies and stepfamily life all the more challenging to examine. And yet they have become the most widespread form of living structure in this country today.[2]

Though my own experiences of being in a stepfamily are unique, I find in talking with individuals, both adults and children who are members of a stepfamily, there are some common threads and themes which run throughout. Frequently what is most common is meeting complicated situations and unexpected emotions abruptly and head on. The more I work with people, the more I wonder: What is a "family" today? Even more importantly: What is a "stepfamily"? Curiously, the latter word is not included in standard American dictionaries though stepmother, stepfather, and stepchildren are. This is more than strange considering the growing number of stepfamilies in this country and around the world and the fact that stepfamilies and extended families are today's reality; they are *not* the anomaly but most decidedly the norm.

We now have many euphemisms for stepfamilies: remarried, recreated, reconstituted, recoupled, acquired, binocular, second family, non-nuclear family, non-biological family, blended.[3] But those living in a stepfamily know they can be anything *but* blended in the sense of being mixed together smoothly. For some nothing could be farther from the truth. Put too many different colors together simultaneously and you may be in for some surprises, not all of which are pleasant. Frequently there are painful adjustments to be made in stepfamily life for which we are not adequately prepared—if we are prepared at all. Stepfamilies can hurt in a lot of places, and it is important to address this and the confusion which often results after remarriage with open eyes, even more importantly with open hearts.

What about the word "stepparent?" This now comes in so many variations that it is difficult to keep track of them all, but at least greeting card companies are beginning to acknowledge that we stepparents exist. Some variations include my dad's new wife; my mom's new husband; my ex's new mate; or my former partner's spouse. These all avoid the "step" prefix entirely as if there were something vaguely wrong and disturbing about the label. How many of us who are in a stepfamily have felt momentarily ill at ease when introducing our stepchildren or our stepchildren introducing us as "that other person"? There is an awkwardness and feeling of strangeness that for some, perhaps many, never goes completely away. I used to wonder about my stepdaughter: What should I call you? What should you call me? What should *I* call me? Where do we all fit in?

None of this linguistic maneuvering changes the fact that there can be many difficult adjustments involved in stepfamily creation and formation. We receive scant training how to be biological parents and even less (if any) about being stepparents. I learned from my mother, for better or for ill, how to be a mom. I never learned how to be a *step*mom. When I grew up, there were few, if any, role models to emulate in this regard. The World War II generation stayed married; it was up to us Baby Boomers to radically change the marriage mold. Like many parents who are stepparents today, I found myself groping in uncharted territory having had no examples from my own upbringing upon which to base or understand this new breed of family life.

Stepfamily and family are not only different words; they are different worlds. It is difficult to appreciate prior to the fact how much stepfamily life can be founded upon hurt and loss and how much confusion, anger, and misunderstanding may be involved in the early evolution of stepfamily relationships. This certainly is not true for everyone living in a stepfamily. The potential, however, for such problems is greater due to the dissolution and reorganization of family members in new and novel ways and the fact that the original family unit did not work out as hoped for or planned. As my stepdaughter said: somehow it is easier to comprehend the death of a person than it is to understand the death of love. For some the dissolution of the original family may be what they want; for others, children in particular, it may be their worst fear. The birthing of a new family and new community by remarriage can require a great deal of time, additional coping skills, and more patience to realize for the mutual benefit of all.

I feel that part of the difficulty in discussing stepfamilies is that it often means talking about feelings that are painful to admit to and even more so to share. Jealousy, anger, hurt, resentment: not a particularly inviting picture of the second (or third) time around. Yet learning how to look at and spot the trouble before it gets unwieldy is particularly necessary for successful stepfamily living because in many cases this family path is born out of pain and loss as much, if not more so, as the hope for a second chance to get things right. This protracted painfulness does not necessarily apply to all who say "I do" a second time. But living in a stepfamily is a challenge in learning what needs changing and molding in character—for all members of the extended family—and what needs to be accepted with love.

In my work with individuals and couples, I haven't heard many describe stepfamily life as a thoroughly wonderful experience. But I also remind myself that people seek my help when things are not running smoothly in their stepfamily situations. More often I hear words like "the exact opposite of what I expected." This is hardly an encouraging description of marriage the second time for either the adults *or* the children involved. There are many individuals who experience shock and numbness when they marry someone who already has a child or children of his or her own. This also includes the children who become part of the new marriage. Those who remarry often wonder: "What's going on here? I thought we were going to be happy." Sometimes the exact opposite occurs at the beginning.

At times it feels as if stepfamilies somehow share a common story that each member is trying to get out amidst croaks, sour notes, and mismatched rhythms and timing. One of the reasons stepfamily life can be so challenging is that it frequently entails dealing with ambivalent loyalties and feelings of abandonment and betrayal. It is not uncommon for many stepfamily members to experience these difficult emotions for quite some time. But paradoxically the ambivalence and negative feelings can also provide the vehicle for learning how to pull through the trials and tribulations which are unique to stepfamily life.

Many people today are experiencing the transition of living between different families, parents, worlds, and ways of being. Perhaps there are those who wonder what to do or what is going on when it is the stepfamily situation itself that presents many of these problems. So keep in mind:

Stepparenting Without Guilt Rule #1

You cannot take away the pain of the past or pretend it's not real. Recognize and accept stepfamily problems for what they are and know that in most stepfamilies the best way to achieve genuine bonding is to work through the hard times.

SOME FACTS AND FIGURES

Perhaps stepfamilies have not received the legitimacy they deserve because of our tentative and ambivalent feelings about them in general. Even though it is not today's reality, we still hold the nuclear family and "'til death do us part" as an ideal. What is it about the word "step" that feels so disruptive and sad? For one thing, it means we have failed once at living happily ever after. The prefix itself comes from the old English word "steop" which means bereaved, orphaned, or deprived.[4] In the past most people who remarried were widowed, but circumstances now are quite different. In 1900 almost 90% of all stepchildren became so through the loss of one or both of their biological parents; less than a century later this is true for only about one-third. This reflects a trend toward stepfamilies and non-traditional family structures by choice, not by death. Now more Americans are part of a second family than a first, and this may be an underestimation of the true picture because statistics do not include unmarried couples living together with children or same sex couples sharing parenthood and stepparenthood.[5]

Approximately thirty-five million people now live in stepfamilies with thirteen hundred new ones forming *each day*.[6] About half a million adults in the United States become stepparents every year, and 15 million children under the age of 18 grow up in this type of family.[7] Three out of every five divorces involve children, and within five years of this initial divorce, 75% of these individuals remarry, making a large number of individuals into stepparents and stepchildren every year.[8] This means that the role of stepparent is becoming increasingly important and pervasive as our society undergoes continuing marital evolution.

Though this is true, many of us still perceive the nuclear family as the standard in our society because it represents the way we Americans *think* families should be rather than how they truly are. Although we are witnessing its demise, many people still hold the traditional nuclear family as their model for action and behavior. A number of individuals involved in non-nuclear families still want to be perceived as "normal," the implication being that somehow stepfamilies are not. At the very least something went wrong, otherwise they wouldn't be in a stepfamily. Though in transition, this feeling of difference still is held by many. According to one survey of stepfamily life:

> The answers [of stepfamily members] . . . clearly reflected the subjects' preoccupation and anxiety about being considered a traditional family. This was the outstanding reaction. . . . What counted was that they should not appear "different" from whatever they believed was the "typical" American family.[9]

The underlying assumption is that stepfamily life and step relationships are not as good as intact families, and there is some evidence to support this view.[10] Research studies show that stepchildren have more developmental, emotional, and behavioral difficulties than children from intact families and often form the highest proportion of those in need of professional help for emotional and behavioral problems.[11] Sadly, stepchildren are also more likely to be the victims of abuse.[12] This may have less to do with the experience of stepfamily life per se as it has to do with individuals' attitudes and prejudices toward this form of living. It also points to the fact that many people simply have not been taught the additional coping tools and interpersonal skills they need to make an easier transition to a second or third family.

I feel that one of the reasons it is so easy to deny certain aspects of stepfamily living is that it becomes a way of covering up how painful an experience it can be. We come to know things about other people's lives that under different circumstances we would never know or even want to. Things such as financial disagreements and emotional difficulties become our business because we become involved in a wider constellation of lives, a different kind of family and community. Stepfamilies, more so than biological families, continue to reconstitute like a kaleidoscope. At the beginning that restructuring can be hard, and knowing this prior to the fact can help.

STEPFAMILY STYLES AND TYPES

As difficult as it may be to answer the question "What is a family?", I think it is more confusing still to answer the question "What is a stepfamily?" Is it:

- Children living with their remarried parent and stepparent?
- Families in which a child lives with a single biological parent but visits his or her remarried biological parent and stepparent?
- Families in which the couple is not married but have children from previous relationships either living with them or visiting?
- A couple with only those children who actually live with them and not those who visit them?
- A stepmother with no children plus a father with his kid(s)?
- A stepfather with no children plus a mother with her kid(s)?
- A couple who bring children into the remarriage and then have children of their own?
- A couple who bring children into the marriage, making them both biological parents and stepparents, but have no children together?[13]

Sound confusing? With good reason. Stepfamily life presents many unique challenges stemming from a number of different factors, the most immediate one being all the possible combinations of people. The myriad stepfamily permutations can be mind-boggling depending upon the number of people involved; the behavior styles of stepparents and stepchildren; the distances between the various households; whatever custodial and financial arrangements are in place between extended family members; the number of previous marriages; and the number of children involved from each marriage. To say that disorganization and miscommunication can achieve new levels of confusion and frustration in stepfamily life is an understatement. There are so many different parent/child constellations and combinations that some researchers actually came up with twenty-six different stepfamily arrangements, each with its own advantages and disadvantages.[14] Knowing beforehand that confusion is the rule may help make transitioning into a stepfamily easier. Flexibility is the key.

Stepparenting Without Guilt Rule #2

A future stepparent needs to assess the many stepfamily variables before entering into an agreement. Do not abdicate personal responsibility to educate yourself about the ins and outs of stepfamily life. This does not necessarily mean you will decide against remarriage, but at least you will have a clearer picture of what you are getting yourself into.

MYTHS AND MISCONCEPTIONS

Other obstacles that prevent us from looking at stepfamily life more objectively are all the myths and misconceptions we have evolved in our efforts to make the stepfamily experience more palatable. Some of the more common ones include:

- Stepfamilies are the same and function the same as nuclear families.

This is not so. The first few years of stepfamily life generally have much more conflict, confusion, boundary testing, and acting-out behavior than intact families. Trying to imitate the traditional nuclear family may actually hinder the development of stepfamily relationships.

• The death of a spouse makes stepfamily formation and stepparenting easier.

Not necessarily. It depends upon the individuals involved and the emotional and psychological impact of divorce. After losing a parent, young children may view remarriage as a betrayal, and unresolved grief can create additional problems in the new stepfamily.

• Stepchildren are easier to deal with when they do not live in your home.

Again, not always so. In the early years of our stepfamily experience it was quite the opposite. A visiting stepchild who comes and goes can be quite disruptive. Feelings of anxiousness and nervousness may arise every time you wait for him or her to arrive. This also applies to other members of the stepfamily as well as the stepchild as she/he comes and goes. (Exits and reentry form a sub-category all their own in stepfamily life which I will talk about later.)

• "Oh, so and so won't be that much a part of my life. What's a little weekend every now and then?" (Otherwise known as a full-blown case of the I-Can-Handle-It Syndrome which I will get to later.)

On the contrary. One morning you may wake up wondering: "What is going on here?" Suddenly you realize you sent the wrong tennis shoes home with the wrong child or misplaced the drop off/pick up schedule, which throws you into a stepparenting tizzy.

• "How much trouble can a stepchild be?"

Sometimes a lot. Obviously, this also applies to biological children as well, only with a wider range of possibilities because they live with you all the time.

• "He/she will be just like one of my own children!"

Not so. Stepchildren are not your children, never will be your children, most likely never expect to be, and usually do not want to be your children. This is simply another way of trying to take away feelings of hurt and confusion rather than facing them head-on.

• "I'll show my new husband/wife how much I love him/her by taking care of the children."

This rationale can also be problematic. You may only end up digging yourself an even bigger hole. On a personal note, I was particularly inclined toward this excessive Stepparent Accommodation Disorder—known as SAD—and it was. Sometimes doing less can actually be more effective and powerful.

• "We'll be one great big happy family."

Maybe, maybe not. There are those who traverse the transition to stepfamily life with relative ease; for others, this is not the case at all. Sometimes inappropriate cheerfulness (another facet of the I Can Handle It Syndrome) can generate even more problems because it fails to acknowledge some of the very real difficulties that are present in the formation of stepfamily life.

• Love and respect happen quickly between stepfamily members.[15]

This was not my experience. It can take years of time, patience, and commitment before the harvest of mutual respect can be reaped. And time, patience, and commitment to relationships are qualities which our society does not inherently value or nourish with its quick fix, if it doesn't work out, move on mentality. Relational skills, parenting skills, and stepparenting skills take time and need to be learned. Good relationships are not accidental. They do not arise automatically or by magic. They are the result of perseverance, patience, and a lot of hard work.

SYNCOPATED LIVING RHYTHMS

Over and above our preconceived notions about stepfamily life, there is an artificial time frame generated by the stepfamily experience which can further complicate matters. Members of stepfamilies do not have the opportunity to evolve their own story, especially at the beginning. In a traditional family structure, marriage usually comes first, followed by a period in which the two people are a couple, then have children. In stepfamilies, however, the reverse is true. The two major events in life, marriage and birth, are spliced together rather than spread out over time. Biological parents are able to learn on the job and grow (hopefully) in their parenting ability as their off-spring develop. Stepparents do not have the luxury of bonding in the same way; there is little or no time to prepare for the immediate and often numerous adjustments that are required in stepfamily life. From my own experience, my husband and I came home after our wedding ceremony and argued where my stepdaughter would put her sleeping bag. I later learned from others that this is not such an unusual event.

As much as biological off-spring challenge and change a marriage, at least there are nine months to prepare for their arrival. And even then it is not enough to begin to fathom how your life alters with the advent of children. But with ready-made children the impact is immediate. Stepfamilies form through disruption, time pressures, and reintegration which can be an odd and lurching process at best. Individual members must exert a conscious effort to establish their own identity. Knowing who's on first truly becomes a refined form of stepparenting art because this type of family life frequently is much lumpier and less predictable than intact family situations.

Being in a stepfamily requires that we stepparents function in a different way. Immediately after "I do" we often are expected to perform but we are not necessarily given the requisite tools to do so. It's not as if your stepchild (or stepparent) comes with a brochure or operation manual, although he or she is already made. This is true of biological children and intact families, but problems of ignorance and inexperience are compounded in stepfamily life by the sheer number of people involved. This difference alone many times means the difference between success and failure in stepfamily relationships. Unfortunately, too often many of us learn this after the fact.

The impulse, however, is for stepfamilies to model intact families because that is what most of us who are stepparents experienced while growing up (on television at least). Being in a stepfamily means learning how to negotiate by a different set of rules. This is something most of us raised in traditional family structures did not anticipate because our own childhood led us to have certain notions about family life and the way families are. We learned about family by being in a family, but most of us did not learn about being in a *step*family. Different coping and communication skills are required and need to be learned. Low cohesiveness and less togetherness may actually aid stepfamily formation and bonding because we all need time and space, especially psychological space, to sort things out.[16] Again, a different rhythm is called for.

Stepparenting Without Guilt Rule #3

Be prepared from the beginning that stepfamilies do not function the same as intact, nuclear families. If you expect them to do so, you may experience even more trouble. Stepfamilies are their own separate reality and require a different way of life.

UNFINISHED EMOTIONAL BUSINESS

Most stepfamilies generally have to deal with unfinished emotional business brought in from the previous marriage. This emotional baggage can and often does cause disruption. Sadly, and not infrequently, the new marriage does not weather the storm. Stepfamilies make us learn the hard way how precious and tenuous relationships are because things can be so easily upset the second time around. We learn from dissolution and reformation that relationships are not to be taken for granted; they require work and commitment to sustain. In stepfamily life you have to work harder at negotiating, communicating, and resolving conflict, especially when difficult emotions are involved. Arguments about money, child support, time distribution, feelings of territorial invasion, divided attention and assets, jealousy—they are potentially all there and must be addressed if they are.

One of the reasons tension is usually greater in stepfamilies is due to the fact that they tend to be larger (his, hers, yours, mine, and ours) than traditional families.[17] Because of this, the likelihood of role confusion is high, and questions come up over and over again: Which part am I to play? And if I have a part, what is it? This applies to all members of the new family: parent, stepparent, *and* child. Members of a stepfamily, especially stepparents, often feel they are required to act without knowing what the dialogue is or who wrote the script. The undefined role of the stepparent can aggravate this problem which then is compounded by lack of confidence and confusion. We walk on stage in the middle of things without knowing our lines, and yet we are expected to quickly learn how to deal with multiple roles. This holds true for the experience of instant stepchildhood as well.

Another common aspect of unfinished emotional business is the notion that in first marriages we confront our emotional immaturity and the psychological baggage we brought with us from our families of origin. Most of us, however, do not; instead we simply leave the relationship without addressing the underlying emotional dynamics being played out unconsciously between us and our partners. Then we remarry (with or without therapy), and if our new partner has children we have to survive the trauma of instant stepparenthood—as well as overcome the emotional immaturity we did not deal with before. How many of us are unwilling, even loath, to admit having difficulties the second time around? Part of our inner being blurts out: "There must be something wrong with me if I can't get it right *again*!" We often blame ourselves for the problems that arise rather than accepting that the stepfamily situation itself may generate many of them. It is not our fault, nor are we to blame. It is, however, necessary that we take responsibility to inform ourselves about the issues and dynamics involved in our new life.

Sometimes the unfinished emotional business can include that vintage stepfamily guilt inducing clincher (I speak from personal experience here): "Well-you-should-have-known-what-you-were-getting-yourself-into" by well-meaning (or even antagonistic) outsiders when, in fact, there is no way for most of us contemplating remarriage with children to know exactly what is in store. Many of us are afraid to admit these feelings for fear of being admonished with "I told you so!" Then starts the self-flagellation: "Of course, how could I be so naive! I should have known!" But how can you know about something you have never experienced before? There are no stepparenting crystal balls that I am aware of, and yet we punish ourselves for the problems we face as if we should possess some special clairvoyance beforehand. Our expectations usually are high, and when they are not fulfilled, we feel there is something wrong with us. And the thought of failing again I think is more painful and frightening the second time around. This leaves many of us feeling even more discouraged, depressed, and alone; and the sensation of impending disaster can grow like a snowball racing downhill, increasing in size and speed.

For many stepfamilies upheaval of this type, both physical and emotional, can go on for years. When both adults bring children to the new relationship, it may be easier because both sets of children are simultaneously biological children and stepchildren; likewise both parents are biological parents and stepparents. This creates a more balanced situation and generally greater understanding than when only one of the adults has children.

The reality is that for many individuals stepfamily life is harder, and those who remarry need to know of this possibility before saying "I do." We also need to reiterate it to others because it is easily brushed aside in the hopefulness of having a second chance. In stepfamily life the possibilities for communication gaffs and misunderstanding are greater—and that is if the various parties are even talking to one another, which may not be the case. You may have to deal with openly hostile former partners. Or, if people start out with cordial good intentions, this may change as time goes on and problems arise. Trying to deal with differences in life styles; family management skills; people and their personalities; as well as coping with the potential feelings of betrayal, abandonment, jealousy, and anger needless to say can be tough.

Moving through these emotional minefields is a journey most of us would rather not take, and enlightenment of the stepparenting kind can be costly. Where you are in your own psychological, emotional, and spiritual development influences how well you can stepparent. You may discover in remarriage with children what has been called "a journey to emotional adulthood."[18] I know I did. And it is a journey well worth it if you can hang in through the trying and turbulent times.

BEFORE SAYING "I DO"

I have often wondered how many people who become stepparents can anticipate all the painful feelings that may have transpired before their entrance onto the scene? I have also wondered if parents who remarry know what they may be asking of their new lovers in terms of tolerance, compassion, finances, and fair play. I know these issues arise in nuclear families as well, but there is a sense of containment and personal history; of safety, territory, and time which aid the process of nuclear family unfolding. These important components are not available to stepfamilies. Such integration is achieved through committed hard work on the part of all concerned—parents, stepparents, and children alike. And it is important to make the choice of commitment to see the stepfamily through.

You might want to ask yourself before taking the plunge again if you are willing to go through a period of what outsiders might view as protracted warfare to get to the point where you can begin to have a reasonable relationship with the person you love. Are you capable of dealing with his or her children? Stepparenting is a commitment where you need to care for young people for their sake and their sake alone. Sometimes this is hard to remember because one's place and one's role in a stepfamily—whether parent, stepparent, stepchild, or stepsibling—must be earned and worked on; they are not automatic nor are they a given. Remember:

Stepparenting Without Guilt Rule #4

Good relationships can exist without love. They do, however, require consistency and trust. If at first you are unable to experience equity of feeling with your stepchildren, at least concentrate on equity of treatment. Fairness goes a long way toward earning respect.

We face so many questions and unknowns today: the proliferation of nuclear weapons and global armament; environmental demise and decaying cities; the insidious corruption of drugs; and an ersatz culture which champions individualism, consumerism, and winning above community, compromise, and feeling. It takes more than a little faith to bring biological off-spring into such a world, but after nearly twenty years, I believe it requires equal, perhaps even greater, faith and fortitude to become a stepmom or stepdad. By sharing in part my stepfamily experience and story, hopefully what follows will aid others on their own unique stepfamily journey and path.

CHAPTER TWO

Life After Divorce

AFTER DIVORCE, there are those of us who want to be free; those of us who mourn the loss of love; those of us who are angry and vow "never again!"; those of us who might reconsider marriage but not too soon; and those of us who are unsure what we want next. I was in the "not-interested-in-getting-involved-again-too-soon" category. So when a friend of mine and her husband approached me about meeting "this really nice guy," I was unfazed. A blind date over dinner: what could go so horribly wrong? When my friend mentioned this "really nice guy" had a three-year-old daughter, I was even more nonchalant. I remember thinking: we're only talking blind date here, not forever after with children.

Murphy's Law being what it is, of course, I did get involved with "this really nice guy" and we, in fact, did get married. It was then that I plunged headlong into the first of many soon-to-be stepfamily quagmires. New loves and new relationships, especially after a failed first one, are fueled with a seemingly never-ending supply of hope. My efficient mental maneuverings whirred and churned: What could be so horribly difficult about alternate weekends and a month or so during the summer? There would, of course, be a "slight" period of adjustment. Never has a six-letter adjective proved so weighty.

Of course, I did not know that then. Looking back upon it all I can see the maladaptive patterns which were there, but at the time I was clueless. This was years before any professional training in clinical psychology. The only blip that registered on my internal screen was a vague anxiety which I immediately squelched with "I can handle that." My future husband, Peter, later approached me to buy some clothes for my soon-to-be stepdaughter, Nikki, and I thought: at last someone *really* needs me! It warmed the cockles of my soon-to-be stepmother heart when it should have sent warning shivers down my spine.

Having been a school teacher, I considered myself fairly good with children, but Nikki's and my first shopping expedition alone together was a near disaster. She howled incessantly, didn't want to try on any clothes, and talked back to everybody. In utter exasperation, I denied vehemently that she was "my child" (my own children, of course, would never behave so obstreperously!), and walked out of the store in a hurry with Nikki under one arm and a bag of clothes under the other. Yet Nikki was going to be mine, in stepchild form at least, for many years to come. And that was a failure of understanding on my part, blinded at the time by anger, ignorance, confusion, and fear. Not a very auspicious beginning for either of us, especially when I felt I was just trying "to do the right thing." Which leads me to a particularly relevant point:

Stepparenting Without Guilt Rule #5

Beware of stepparent dogooderism. You cannot change the past, and you may make things harder for yourself by trying to "make things better" or "set things right." Sometimes being a good stepparent requires knowing the virtue of restraint.

It took a while for that to sink in because one of the biggest challenges you face as a stepparent is often the feeling of impotence and powerlessness over what is going on. You are the newcomer, not the former partner and child(ren). They are the preexisting system which you join. If you do not know how to take care of yourself and your own needs, when to back off or when to stand firm, you may be in for trouble. This can be one of the most painful lessons stepfamily life has to teach us because boundaries are tenuous in this form of living and can be easily blurred if not carefully defined. Moreover, often former spouses and the children involved are hurt and angry themselves and less than cooperative about new living arrangements. But in uncharted, previously unexplored emotional waters sometimes the stepfamily boundaries do not get erected until after the fact. When you finally do get them established, they need to be held. This, too, can be difficult and draining.

On several occasions I approached Peter and admitted quite frankly that getting married again was problematic enough, but stepparenthood felt beyond me. Then came another vintage stepparenting clincher which may sound familiar: "Don't worry, honey. I'll take care of everything. You won't have to deal with any of it. *Haven't I been a single parent all these years?*"

The answer is both yes and no. Sometimes a single parent has fulltime responsibility for the caring and raising of a child; sometimes not. And while all custody and visitation arrangements are unique, they are also subject to change once a new stepparent enters the scene. This is something I failed to consider, or even to think about.

I believe it is part of human nature to want to believe in our power to effect change, to make things better, to lend a hand, and to reexperience love. Denial can be very well intentioned at times, but it still is what it is: not looking at and accepting the unvarnished truth. Certainly this does not apply to all stepparenting and stepfamily situations. Yet it is better to know the possibility that changes and problems may occur than to expect that they won't. This leads me to another important point:

Stepparenting Without Guilt Rule #6

Question the natural parent when he or she promises to "take care of everything." No matter how sincere and well intentioned your future spouse may be, practically speaking, it may not work out that way in day-to-day reality. In stepfamily life some healthy skepticism may be necessary for self-preservation.

Since that time and over the intervening years, I have wondered how much experience and background help with parenting, whether biological or step. Each child is so different, so unique that being a successful parent or stepparent is akin to playing a complicated piece of music. There are so many different notes, permutations, and combinations of sound that all you can hope to do is practice a lot, maintain a nimble soul, and pray fervently that everything comes together harmoniously in the end—which in family and stepfamily life can be some twenty years down the road. This requires a great deal of dedication, patience, and love.

STEPFAMILY ROLES

Because of the challenges I faced in the early years of my remarriage, I spent considerable time and effort learning more about stepfamily life. I discovered there are many ways individuals involved in this type of family may respond to the new situation they find themselves in. Take, for instance, the following stepparenting styles:[1]

• The Superstepparent—those who try to play the role of the perfect parent (stepmothers are particularly prone to this). The superstepmom or superstepdad may also be known as the competitor; i.e. trying to beat out the biological parent at who is best. The smotherer is a similar variation on this style because they try do too much.

• The Rescuer—stepparents who believe their stepchildren have not had the proper care, love, and/or discipline, etc. and are determined to "make things better." This is another problematic syndrome afflicting stepmothers predominantly, though stepfathers exhibit this as the disciplinarian and/or dictator (see below). Akin to the rescuer is the stepparent who is in denial about all the tough spots that may be there in stepfamily life. For this type of stepparent, everything is always good (a.k.a. inappropriate cheerfulness). This type of stepparenting calls for caution.

• The Dictator—those stepparents who enforce the rules. Stepfathers are more inclined to this because they feel they should have the last word in family matters. Experience demonstrates, however, that whichever sex the dictator appears in, it is problematic at best and doomed to failure at worst. Stepfamilies require firmness but not rigidity. Frequently due to our own inexperience or fear we stepparents forget this fact.

• The Reluctant One—this stepparent is the flip-side of the dictator. He or she wants to make a good impression and get along with his/her stepchildren but is fearful of making mistakes and often vacillates when it comes to setting rules, regulations, and boundaries. This, too, can cause problems.

• The Ignorer—those stepparents who are detached and have little or nothing to do with their stepchildren. Stepparents may also combine these various roles or switch back and forth between them when feeling stressed and/or unsure of themselves.

Aside from different stepparenting styles, there are numerous stepchild types which must be factored into the equation as well. If you remarry someone who has an infant or toddler, these children require the most physical supervision and can be exhausting, but at least you become part of their lives early on. They may, or may not, accept you more readily into their world. But you also take on the stepparenting job longer and may have to deal with more hostilities, confusion, and insecurity due to their age.

The second group involves the 4 to 10 year olds. They usually do not require the same intense physical care and supervision as the first group and may not, or may, be bothered by issues of loyalty and guilt. However, they do require that stepparents formulate specific rules and standards, what is and is not acceptable behavior, and the necessity of taking up the disciplinary gauntlet. This is not an easy task in any parenting situation, step or otherwise. The socialization of children requires a lot of hands on activity and energy, something which can challenge and overwhelm many biological parents, let alone new stepparents.

The third group includes adolescents who traditionally receive a lot of bad parenting press, both biological and step. The fact that they will be out of the home soon does not necessarily make up for all the dirt and disagreement they leave in their wake. It is a challenge indeed to engage in meaningful dialogue with individuals who profess to know everything and who are quite practiced in the art of disdain. Many say this group is the worst, especially for stepmothers.[2]

In addition, stepchildren, like their stepparents, can assume a variety of behavioral approaches once they find themselves in a new family constellation. They can be rude and defiant in order to protect their feelings from further betrayal and hurt. They can voice dislike, view the stepparent as a threat to their biological parent's love; they can come off as aloof, and/or play the peace-maker going between two places. Still others learn how to pit one parent and home off against the other. Two household children can be very adroit at this form of stepfamily manipulation (see the spoiled brat syndrome later). Other stepchildren types include:[3]

- The Condemner or Critic—stepchildren who berate your stepparenting in the absence of their biological parent. They are quite good at pointing out how mean, awful, and/or rotten you are and how much better their real parent is. It is important at such times to remember that these children may be acting this way as a defense against their own feelings of hurt and anger.
- The Pusher—those stepchildren who test limits in order to see how trustworthy and consistent you are. Children in this category may deliberately antagonize and sabotage you in order to get you angry and upset. When we return this behavior in kind due to fatigue, frustration, or whatever it only confirms the wicked stepparent myth in their eyes.
- The Darling—those stepchildren who try to please. Such young people want approval and affection and often are afraid to speak up for their own rights and needs. They may not even know how to begin to do this. The overly good child can also be holding onto anger or fear that disruption could happen again, and being good becomes a way of preventing further pain. This can also lead to manipulative behavior as a way of feeling safe and maintaining the illusion of control in what feels to them like a chaotic world.
- The Pest—there are stepchildren who always seem to be causing problems. Fear of abandonment—an ever-present ghost in many stepfamilies—may lead to difficult behavior, and the need for limit-making can be an unconscious desire for reassurance on their part. It is not unusual

for children of divorce to ask for this over and over again. The whiner and clinger are variations on the pest/insecure stepchild theme and are also related to the pusher.

• The Silent Type—these are stepchildren who do not want to interact with anybody. Their behavior frequently stems from the anxiety that loss could occur another time, and they wish to avoid involvement to combat this possibility. Or these children may have been overly catered to and pampered by their parents to assuage the latter's guilt. Either way this behavior is debilitating to the child and trying on the stepparent.

• The Wedge—for these stepchildren, the stepparent is decidedly unwelcome, and they may try to break up the new relationship. The uneasy feeling you experience that your stepchild is sabotaging your marriage may not be strange at all but accurate feedback from your environment. As one stepparent says:

> During the early years of my second marriage I remember thinking I was either being a little paranoid or my stepson was trying to break up my marriage. Many years later he admitted he had been trying to break us up. He had plans A, B, C all aimed at making me give up and leave.[4]

These are but a few of the roles and styles we may assume after being thrown into the stew of stepfamily life. The more awareness we can bring, the more conscious choice we can exert as to how we are going to respond. The point is not necessarily to avoid these various behavioral and emotional reactions but to better understand them as they arise.

SPOILED BRAT SYNDROME

Another aspect of stepfamily life that can be quite trying is what I call the spoiled brat syndrome. Though children from intact families certainly can be overly pampered, in stepfamilies the likelihood of the spoiled brat syndrome is even greater. The idea of a stepchild being disadvantaged stems in part from its original meaning of being orphaned and deprived. Though many stepchildren have problems, deprivation frequently is not one of them. Often they are spoiled with gifts and privileges they have not earned to appease the nemesis of stepfamily guilt. Indeed, many family psychologists agree that stepchildren are often spoiled by adults who are trying to compensate for their own feelings of betrayal and abandonment.[5] The label "stepchild" can be used as an excuse to play the victim and escape being held accountable for personal behavior. This fact, coupled with an accompanying lack of consistent rules and responsibilities when moving between two homes, means that stepchildren can easily fall through the disciplinary cracks. As some researchers have noted,

> Biological parents typically make excuses for [their children] because of their own guilt associated with the trauma of divorce. In cases where a youngster can take refuge from one parent's authority by running to the other parent, a child of divorce can avoid discipline . . . almost indefinitely.[6]

Tantrums, bad manners, and provocative behavior may be the result, and this can scare or anger many new stepparents who sincerely are trying to make a positive effort. It is important to remember at these times that stepchildren are going through their own pain and confusion too, perhaps even blaming themselves for the failure of their parents' marriage. This can make them decidedly unlikable and the work of stepparenting more difficult and taxing in the early stages. Even though children do not always like to hear "no," a part of them also wants you to take a stand. This leads me to suggest the following:

Stepparenting Without Guilt Rule #7

The growth of personal responsibility is in inverse proportion to excessive pampering. Giving too much to your stepchild only impedes his or her acquisition of this important adaptive tool. Sometimes less ends up being more because it is important for children to be held accountable for their own behavior.

Regardless of unfortunate past circumstances, a child still has to be responsible for who and what he is, what she does, and how he or she interacts with others. This applies to the adults involved as well. The dynamics of stepfamily life often demand that you step in immediately and do the job. If nobody else previously has set many or any limits in a child's life and the child needs limits, you do what is called for. How long can you afford to wait to be accepted? Your stepchild most likely will fight the discipline, but a failure to act can also be damaging. Over the years I discovered when you are about to waver in matters involving the spoiled brat syndrome, this lucky charm reply helps: "It's fine you do such and such at your other house. In our home we do it *this* way."

Short, honest, and to the point. Demonstrating firmness yet genuine caring at the same time forges the art and practice of being a stepparent. Without this I believe healthy love cannot exist. That doesn't mean this balance is easy to find, and what works for some may not for others. A certain amount of trial and error is required.

INAPPROPRIATE POWER

Inappropriate power and control may also be connected with the spoiled brat syndrome. When we allow children to take over what should be our decisions and responsibilities as parents and adult caretakers, we give them a false sense of power.[7] Frequently parents, and especially stepparents, are frightened of and anxious about their stepchildren, and young people pick up on this intuitively, using it to their advantage. Yet the consequences of this manipulation, whether conscious or unconscious, can be harmful.

What does it communicate to your child or stepchild that you are afraid to say "no" or "yes" due to insecurity or guilt? I will talk more about stepfamily guilt later, but for now it is important to note that it can often get confused with love, and the consequences of this are far-reaching. This abdication of adult responsibility, whether biological or step, can serve to reinforce the spoiled brat syndrome. Children often think they are the reason for their parents' break-up, and this gives them a false sense that they can disrupt the new relationship as well.[8] Here is one example of how manipulative a child can become if allowed to by guilt-ridden adults:

> In one stepfamily . . . seven year old Susan held the power. Susan lived with her mother and stepfather and spent weekends with her father. There was almost no direct communication between the adults in Susan's life, and she carried talks and messages back and forth. . . . Susan would be scheduled to be with her father and she would cry and say she didn't feel well and she didn't want to go. Susan's mother would comfort her daughter . . . [and] cancel the plans she and her husband had made for the day or the weekend, and she would stay home with her daughter. When Susan recovered quickly, her stepfather recognized the manipulative quality of Susan's illness. . . . The relationship between the new couple became strained, and a very vicious downward spiral developed for everyone.[9]

When the adults took charge, Susan's immediate reaction was to have tantrums and complain. But when the grown-ups held firm and went ahead with their plans anyway, she soon settled down. By providing Susan with strong, clearly defined boundaries, she felt better in the long run. It is as if the child is saying: "Do you care enough for me to draw the line? Please put limits around me so I'll know I'm safe." A professional psychologist I know says she used to lie to her friends about being punished by her parents just to prove to them (and herself) that her parents truly cared.

On a personal note, when my husband finally was able to apply the same disciplinary standards to Nikki that he did with our other children, you could almost feel her sigh of relief. I actually overheard her brag the next day to some neighborhood playmates that her daddy finally sent her to her room and made her stay there. Never was a grounding more appreciated by a child—or a stepmom! Being able to act at the right moment gives children a sense of security that they are held and loved. They may not always like this, but as parents and stepparents we must know how necessary it is for our children's well being. If at all possible, work to establish specific regulations and consistent behavioral responses before problems arise. You will find this is a proactive stepparenting measure. Remember:

Stepparenting Without Guilt Rule #8

Stepparenting (and biological parenting) are not about winning a popularity contest. They're about doing the job that is called for, and sometimes that job is tough. Be clear when, where, and on what issues you intend to take a stand.

DISCIPLINE

The spoiled brat syndrome can precipitate another area of stepfamily contention: who takes the disciplinary hand. This is one of the dilemmas you may face in remarriage with children and often right away. Many biological parents want to provide their off-spring with a new parent who will be nurturing, reliable, and give appropriate discipline when needed. Perhaps more than a few single parents remarry so that the new stepparent can help them deal with their ex-spouses over children and relieve them of the harried life of a single mom or dad. In the meantime, the non-custodial parent becomes accustomed to the stepparent being there to help and grows to rely on the stepparent for all the work he or she provides. Some biological parents fall down on the job due to lack of agreement, different disciplinary styles, guilt, or just plain fatigue, and in these cases stepparents frequently fill the void.

I think there may be a certain degree of calculation, consciously or unconsciously, on the part of some individuals looking for a new mate. The new spouse may be tempted to take advantage of the prospective spouse's desire to be helpful and show his/her good intentions. Single parents in search of a husband or wife do not lie or prevaricate necessarily; however, there is the inclination to withhold certain facts and information while the courtship is going on, particularly about difficulties or differences in disciplinary matters. We want so badly to believe that all will be well, or at least better, the second time around; and it is hard to be honest about painful things.

In second marriages the goal for many may not be passionate love as much as it is to find a helpmate and partner who can serve as a good surrogate parent. To *finally* find someone to help may also bring with it an abdication of the biological parent's responsibility. As one stepmother puts it: "[My husband] thought he was finally free to work late and take business trips after our marriage. I felt abused, as if he'd stuck me with *his* chore."[10] Stepparents may also suffer from the disease of the overly obliging, especially stepmothers. We need to learn to accept involvement within the limits of our ability, and this can be a precarious framework to establish. In remarriage with children, it may be necessary to ask a lot of questions. This is one area in life where it actually may be better to anticipate things going poorly at first and then be sincerely grateful if they fair better later on.

The truth is that children from ruptured marriages can feel torn apart because they are pulled in opposite directions. They experience the trauma of going back and forth between two homes which may be openly hostile and where they often are used as pawns between warring ex-partners. Their parents may have stopped loving each other, but that does not mean the children have or that they do not mourn the loss of their original home and family structure. It can be a long and arduous process for children to adjust to the reality of two houses with two different sets of rules; neither right nor wrong, only different.

For the most part, young people know when they are being awful, and there is that part of them which yearns for a grown-up to be a grown-up and create strong walls against which they can butt their heads, learn, and grow. I learned early on that Nikki could call me "mean" as much as she wanted. I didn't like being called that but the consequences of not being firm with her would have been more harmful for both of us in the long run. I was clear about what was and was not acceptable behavior, and the same rules applied to everyone. So in situations calling for stepparents to initiate discipline and limits, I advise the following:

Stepparenting Without Guilt Rule #9

Restraint and patience are important in most instances requiring discipline, but do not hesitate to take appropriate action with your stepchild when called for. Remember that a failure to act can be just as damaging as being overly strict.

How do you go about teaching respect to children, especially stepchildren? For without this, discipline is impossible. You cannot teach it: you must show it, *be* it. Respect and love can often be confused, but without respect, love is difficult to achieve, especially in step relationships. It is surprising how many parents and stepparents are afraid to discipline their children when rightly called for because they do not want their children not to like them. What they fail to understand is that good parenting and especially good stepparenting are not about liking (though we all hope our children will like us someday). They are about *appropriate* parenting: doing what is called for even if the children involved do not like it. Liking isn't the point; doing the job is.

SCHEDULING

Possibly no two words are more loaded in stepfamily life than "the schedule," except perhaps the "ex." Often the schedule is set before the stepparent's entrance onto the scene; sometimes it is not. Or it can change after the fact. Next to money and child support, most custody battles involve how much time each parent is going to have with the children, where they are going to be, who vacations with whom and when. Frequently it is the stepparents, especially stepmoms, who are left to deal with what the courts and biological parents decide.

Holidays and vacations take on new meaning when you are dealing with stepparenthood. So many variables must be considered that at times you feel as if you are conducting an orchestra, trying to satisfy everyone's need to be heard and given voice. The only glitch is someone usually ends up playing a sour note by feeling left out; then hurt and anger seep in, affecting everybody and everything. Trying to cope with these negative feelings is at once difficult and at the same time absolutely necessary. It takes a lot of time, time which under the pressures of the moment we stepparents often feel we do not have.

Part of the friction arises from all the conflicting loyalties. The children of the previous relationship expect "real" Mom and Dad to be there for them just like before (though scheduling arrangements rarely meet this need). The new spouse and children from the remarriage feel that they are the current focus and do not want to be servicing the expectations of the past. This can make for feelings of hurt, betrayal, and guilt in both the former and new family; and the communication mix-ups around scheduling and visits between even well-meaning parents and stepparents can be endless. Depending upon how many different parties are involved, dozens of people can be affected by the realities—and vagaries—of stepfamily life. As one person comments,

> The stepfamily is a tangled web of communication difficulties; stepparent and stepchild, stepparent and spouse (stepchild's parent), stepparent and absent parent, parent and absent parent, parent and child, child and absent parent; not to mention the extended family of aunts, uncles, and grandparents. Any one problem and the whole household feels the negative effects and ramifications.[11]

In scheduling matters, I have found it helpful to present a united front by supporting my spouse before stepchild and "ex." You can always negotiate later in private about vacations, holidays, and other plans. It is equally important not to take out your anger and frustration at such trying situations on your stepchild. Once when our plans were changed due to lack of timely communication between Nikki's parents, I decided that no matter how angry I might be at them for mix-ups and confusion, it was neither Nikki's fault nor her responsibility. This helped my relationship with my stepdaughter a great deal. As Nikki herself said: the last thing children moving between two homes need to think is that something else went wrong due to their fault. Both stepparents and biological parents need to be sensitive to this fact.

As mentioned earlier, entries and exits are a specific subcategory of stepfamily scheduling which carry their own unique emotions and challenges. They generally occur around weekends and vacations as part of the schedule, and they are also the time when most problems usually occur. Here is one stepmother's view:

> A pattern emerged: a noisy confrontation on some issue, usually shortly before Bill [stepchild] was to return to his mother. Even though we recognized the pattern, and I would resolve weekly not to be drawn into a confrontation, Bill would find a chink in my armor and "push my button."[12]

This sounds familiar to me as well. In the early years of our stepfamily life, it felt as if Nikki would become involved in an obligatory fight or some sort of emotional eruption whenever she arrived on Friday afternoon or before she left on Sunday evening. My maternal hot button would be set off when I watched her bossing around her half-siblings or ignoring them altogether: I inwardly cringed and then became angry as I saw the scene unfold. These behaviors on Nikki's part no doubt were due largely to insecurity and the understandable frustration she felt at having to switch homes twice a week. I can only imagine the number of stepfamily weekends or gatherings soured by a similar sequence of events.

One of the things that proved useful for us was to have a neutral place, such as school or a nearby MacDonald's, for dropping off and picking up between visits. Or if you drop off and pickup at your stepchild's house, it helps to make the change over cordial but brief. I say this because in the early days of a new stepfamily, these transitions can be painful for the children especially. Ask you stepchild what works best for him or her. Do they want you to stay in the car and honk the horn or come to the front door and talk with their biological parent? This is an opportunity to start negotiating what works best for the both of you.

It also helps before exiting to make sure that your stepchild has all of his or her possessions and belongings gathered together and ready to go by the front door. If your stepchildren have a specific outfit or clothes to leave in, make sure they go home in them clean, even if they arrived in them dirty. Little things like this can help make the transition between homes move more smoothly. As time goes on and a routine gets established, entries and exits generally prove less daunting.

STEPSIBLINGS

Another aspect to consider in remarriage with children is how to deal with stepsibling interaction since the relationships between the various children of remarriage can represent many challenges. You may be in a stepfamily where you have no biological children of your own and have no biological children with your new mate. This is a stepfamily with only stepchildren and no half-siblings. Stepsiblings and half-siblings, however, further alter the stepfamily equation. In my own case, I have one stepchild and three biological children, and all four children are half-siblings. Half-siblings generally are thought to have a positive rather than negative effect on stepfamily relations because there is the biological link that you and your stepchild do not share. [13] This, however, can also generate additional feelings of territoriality and jealousy over divided parental attention and assets. But trust me on this one: siblings—whether whole, half, or step—can and will argue, and this bickering is among the most trying aspects of family and stepfamily life. As several researchers write,

> Stepsiblings problems become so complex they can be mind-boggling. The remarried partners more than likely never

> imagined how much of a drain the children's problems would put on their relationship. Some second marriages end in divorce, not because of a husband and wife breakup, but from the desire to remove themselves from all the new problems that have come up because of the children.[14]

At times divorce feels as if it is the only escape route from having to cope with all the stepsibling logistics and infighting. Many people who remarry are willing to risk the marriage itself in order not to have to deal with the children. Again, not a very auspicious note upon which to sound a second chance. Knowing that you may be in for some rough stepparenting seas in this regard can help you draw upon additional resources of patience when stepsiblings argue. Time-outs and physical separation may be necessary. Peace at any price may not be appropriate, but a quiet cooling off period can help everybody when stepfamily temperatures rise.

Stepsiblings also change the birth order, and this can affect stepfamily dynamics as well. In one family your child may be the oldest and in your stepfamily he or she may lose this privileged position. (As Nikki pointed out on numerous occasions: she had to remind everyone who was First Kid.) Barring physical violence, bullying, and psychological intimidation, parents and stepparents need to let step and halfsibs work things out for themselves. Letting them sort it out, however, is often far easier said than done because it can be hard to stand back and watch the step and half relationships noisily unfold. But just remember: if it is okay for you not to like your children and stepchildren all the time, it is also okay for them not to like each other. This does not mean that they are allowed to beat up on one another, but they do have the right not to care. As mentioned earlier, psychological and emotional space may be even more important in stepfamilies when children from different backgrounds are brought together and must learn how to interact. There is also the possibility of increased sexual interest among step-siblings which may need to be monitored.

There are some positive outcomes to the stepsib dynamic, if you are patient. Recent studies show that children who learn how to adjust to stepfamily situations can adapt to other situations in life better than children from traditional family structures.[15] This is one of the plusses of the stepfamily experience. You need to remind yourself of this as you look out upon what may be a difficult stepsibling scene.

Stepparenting Without Guilt Rule #10

Know the virtue (and necessity) of accepting what you cannot change and work from there. Do not try to fix everything all at once, especially with step-siblings. Genuine positive regard and love cannot be achieved overnight where children of remarriage are concerned.

One of the things I am the most proud of as a parent and stepparent is that all four of our children can honestly look at one another's strengths and weaknesses and accept them for who and what they are. They (and we) have learned to work together as a team, and this is one of the positive outcomes of our stepfamily experience.

CHAPTER THREE

Period of Adjustment

THE BEGINNING YEARS of stepparenting and remarriage are often referred to as a "period of adjustment." Though every family, biological or blended, is unique in its own way, there are some fairly predictable stages in stepfamily development.[1] Knowing about them can help make new stepparents and stepchildren feel less alone and vulnerable to what at times feels chaotic and out-of-control.

During the honeymoon or fantasy stage of an approaching remarriage everybody tries to make a good impression. Usually both children and adults are relatively happy about the idea of a "new" family; things move along fairly well as the individuals get to know one another and plan for their life together. This usually means everyone is involved in his or her own version of happily ever after or have succumbed to unbridled I-Can-Handle-It optimism.

This is followed by the next stage where disillusionment and negative feelings begin to arise. For our stepfamily, this happened fairly quickly. During this phase, things do not work out as everyone had hoped and a sense of being trapped begins to emerge, along with feelings of resentment, particularly within the new stepparent. ("This isn't how I imagined things would be!") Depression can rear its head, along with a sense of helplessness about not being able to do anything about it. Fear of failure grows as the foibles and idiosyncrasies of each family member come forth. This stage of trying emotional experiences can last for years. And that's the good news because many stepfamilies never get through this part of the period of adjustment; they collapse under the pressure and negativity of it all.

In the next confrontational stage, things come to a head. Someone (usually but not limited to the stepparent) cannot hide his or her feelings any longer, repressed emotions explode, and open hostility occurs. A variation on this stage is a series of crises, oscillating back and forth in rapid succession. However, if the individuals can express their feelings and are willing to talk about what is bothering them, there is some hope for working out the interpersonal problems and conflicts.

This brings me to the last stage in the period of adjustment: reevaluation and decision-making. After the turmoil and dust have settled, stepfamily members must decide whether or not they want to stay together and keep on trying or give it up as a bad job and throw in the towel. Even if only one member of the stepfamily remains recalcitrant, disharmony and discord will continue, along with disillusionment and confrontation. Regaining equilibrium requires that each member believes in one another at least enough to have some faith they will make it as a family, albeit in a different form than they have been used to or have fantasized about. In many cases this period of adjustment can be quite difficult and protracted. Says one stepparent:

> I have not gotten beyond the adjustment period yet. It is entirely possible that the adjustment period never ends, and I am here thinking about the beginning of the constant reshuffling that will occupy the rest of our lives.[2]

This may make many pause. The average period of adjustment for most stepfamilies is five years, but it can and often does extend longer.[3] In our own case, it took quite a while to establish a workable stepfamily rhythm.

FAIRY TALES DON'T COME TRUE

During the more trying times of our early period of adjustment, Nikki's favorite movie was "Little Orphan Annie" and her favorite story "Bad Mousie" from *The Tall Book of Make-Believe*.[4] She insisted that I read "Bad Mousie" to her several times a week.

In this story there is a mother, her daughter named Donnica, and a scalawag mouse who gets into all sorts of trouble with scissors, glue, mud, etc. Bad Mousie is not a mean-spirited or malicious creature; it is simply that nobody has taken the time to teach him how to be good. Donnica's mother, however, does not find Bad Mousie at all amusing and after numerous ignored warnings to change his ill-mannered ways, she ties his tail to an umbrella and sends him off on a puff of wind. Bad Mousie lands in much harsher climes, gets cold and wet, and begins to miss Donnica, her mother, and their warm, cozy cottage.

After assorted trials and tribulations, Bad Mousie, sadder but wiser, finds his way back to Donnica. The mother wants no part of Mousie but Donnica intercedes, promising her mother that she will take it upon herself to teach Bad Mousie how to be good, and Mousie promises to try. With patient effort and perseverance Donnica instructs Bad Mousie on the finer points of household cleanliness and etiquette (e.g. wiping mud off his tiny paws, folding his napkin, picking up his messes). During this tutelage his oft-repeated refrain is: "And I will try to be good!" (Donnica also kisses Bad Mousie a lot to help him be good faster.) In the end, Donnica's protestations soften her mother and she relents. Mousie is allowed to stay as a full-fledged member of the household, Donnica gains a new friend, and as is wont in most fairy tales, they live happily ever after. This bears little resemblance to real life.

For a while Nikki called me Donnica (when she wasn't calling me mean), and on some level she knew I was trying to help her with hugs and kisses and time-outs to teach her some of the things she sensed she needed to know. But this was hard on us both: she often resisted and I often resented the task. When it *finally* sank in that this stepfamily business—at least my version of it—was qualitatively and quantitatively different from the type of family experience I had had before, I was some six years into our marriage. Talk about adjustment! Previously to this, I had never thought of myself as a particularly slow learner, but when I became a stepparent I suddenly was rendered inexplicably and hopelessly dumb. It made me think in hindsight how I abdicated my own responsibility in learning more about stepfamily life and the people I would become involved with prior to remarriage. I had no one to hold accountable for that lack of questioning other than myself. I simply had been too naïve and trusting and engaged in a fair amount of I Can-Handle-It denial about what might be in store.

REUNION FANTASY

One of the key factors influencing the period of adjustment is what I call the reunion fantasy. Many children cope with the split between their parents, even though that coping may have nothing whatsoever to do with their liking it. Some separations are amicable, others quite acrimonious; yet many youngsters continue to grieve for some time after their parents have adapted to their new adult life. This was not only my own personal experience but also what I have witnessed working with children from divorced homes. We hear, or maybe we choose to believe, that children of divorce and separation are happy because it lessens the adults' guilt and their desire to move on. We argue that children adapt much more readily, that they are resilient and bounce back, etc.

But there is something rather self-serving for us grown-ups in this "they'll adjust" attitude. For many youngsters, it is as if something still is missing, some quiet pain yet lurking behind the door of their hearts. The truth of the matter is that children can harbor the fantasy that Mommy and Daddy will miraculously reunite for years, even after both biological parents have remarried or long gone their separate ways.[5] A colleague, divorced for over twenty years, told me once that her son still harbors some distant, wispy thoughts of "my mom" and "my dad" getting back together again.

In my own case, I remember Nikki bursting into tears one night in her bedroom crying, "I don't understand why my Mommy and Daddy can't be together!" This was over three years into our marriage. Her mother had by then remarried, and there was some hope on my part that things would begin to calm down. She looked at me pleading, not angry this time but deeply hurt and confused. "Why don't you marry my stepfather so Mommy and Daddy can be together again?" This followed a child's exquisite logic: the stepparent should marry the stepparent and the biological parent remarry the biological parent, matching up the words and label: step joining step, nature with nature. Obviously a child's wishes and an adult's actions do not always so neatly mesh. Children often blame themselves for their parents' split, or they continue to dream of their parents coming together again, and we stepparents often bear the brunt of these defeated longings. In the moment of Nikki's tearful plea all I could do was give her a big hug and feel for her sadness. Sometimes being a stepparent means witnessing someone else's pain in compassionate silence and that can be hard.

How many children are going to be grateful to you for marrying one of their parents and disrupting their primary foundation or dashing the fantasy of their parents reuniting? How many children are going to thank you for splitting up their home and security (even if that happened years ago), perhaps making them switch schools, friends, maybe even towns? Remarriage destroys their dream of things going back the way they used to be, even if the way it used to be wasn't all that wonderful. No child is going to be happy about that.

Those of us who marry people with children need to appreciate that the psychological effects of separation and divorce can unfold for quite some time. Follow-up studies done on adolescents from divorced homes found that even years later many still regarded their parents' divorce as a major event, if not *the* major event, in their lives.[6] This certainly is not true for everyone, but it is a possibility for some, if not many, children of divorce. What makes their parents happy does not necessarily make young people feel the same way; quite often the children's feelings are the exact opposite. Here is one version of remarriage from a teenager's point of view:

> I was fourteen and about to go into the ninth grade when my parents divorced. Sara, my little sister, went to live with Mom, but she came home for a visit at Thanksgiving. That's when Dad popped the news; for Christmas we were getting a new mother. Sara thought it was wonderful. She would be able to live with us. She and Dad laughed and cried and babbled about how great a person Rita is. I just asked to be excused, went to my room and tried to read.
>
> The day Dad married Rita was the worst day of my life. I kept feeling homesick, only I couldn't go home and be all

> right, because I was at home. The house was full of people. . . . Sara hung onto Rita nearly the whole time. She even asked, "Can I call you Mommy, now?" . . . It made me sick. I could tell my Dad expected me to be jumping for joy, too, like everybody else. But I wasn't.
>
> I was mad. Mad at Dad for being a traitor to my Mom. Mad at Mom for going off to law school and leaving us alone. Mad at the two brats, Rita's kids, who were going to come live in our house. Mad at Sara for liking them and their mother. But most of all, I was mad at Rita. . . .
>
> My grandparents took me home with them that night and I stayed a week while Dad and "my new mother," as Grandma called her, went on their honeymoon. "But I don't want a new mother," I told Grandma. "I already have one!" . . . I hated the word stepmother. And I hated the word stepchild even more. . . .
>
> [When I went home], I saw right away that it wasn't my house anymore. It was [Rita's]. . . . Suddenly, I was afraid to look in my bedroom, and was even more horrified when I did. . . . I blew up. I told Rita I didn't like her and her kids marching in and taking over like that. And she told me this was now their house too. Pretty soon we were yelling at each other. She called me a spoiled brat. I called her an ugly stepmother. Then I ran out of the house. . . .[7]

Often children can try consciously or unconsciously to get their parents back together again, and the first step, of course, is to break up the new marriage. Sometimes the natural parents may reunite for a while, and the child may get an unrealistic sense of his or her power in such situations.[8] Or the grown-ups move on trying the best they can to reorganize their lives and frequently do not understand why their children don't like the new parent or stepfamily. As some researchers note,

> It may seem like a statement of the obvious to stress how important it is that the adults involved be aware of this [that children's developmental needs do not necessarily change to fit remarriage], but it is perhaps equally obvious that it is

> easier said than done. The parent who has found a new partner and is looking to the future with renewed happiness and optimism is . . . least likely to be able to see the situation through the eyes of the children as . . . an uncertain, unwelcome or even threatening change.[9]

ESCAPE FANTASY: DIVORCE

As our period of adjustment teeter-tottered between okay and awful, I found myself considering divorce simply so I would not have to deal with Nikki anymore (or her mom and new stepdad). That was my escape fantasy—a grim reverse parallel to the reunion fantasy of many children. I imagined that by leaving I would rid myself of my husband's "ex," her new mate, *and* their child. This might confirm my wickedness as a stepmother, but at least I thought there would be some relief for me. One is so tempted to assume the position: "Well, if this doesn't work I can always leave," because quite frequently it may be easier momentarily to bail out than see things through. This is not what you would call a good working foundation for marriage *or* remarriage.

In stepparenting you confront many difficult choices:

If you choose yourself and your own needs, your children may suffer. If you choose the children and their needs, you may. Sometimes everyone's needs may be fulfilled if you are lucky, especially in stepfamily life, but this is infrequent at best. Staying together for the sake of your children is a choice and an important one to consider. After deliberation you still may choose to part, but you need to recognize and be prepared for the potential costs involved. As a number of the previous facts indicate, the impact of divorce on many young people is profound, and I wonder how many people who have divorced and remarried have some regrets that they did not try harder the first time around. Leaving and possibly remarrying again might mean signing on for another tour of stepparenting duty, only this time with two or three stepchildren coming along with the package at older, adolescent ages, as well as juggling your own off-spring. The grass, especially in Stepfamily Land, is not always greener. So remember:

Stepparenting Without Guilt Rule #11

First form firm boundaries followed by consistency, appropriate concern, and respect. These are important in any family but absolutely essential in stepfamilies and may help in warding off another divorce.

FEELINGS OF STEPPARENT POWERLESSNESS

The powerlessness I felt during these early stages of our remarriage adjustment was debilitating, and I suspect other stepparents in these circumstances experience similar feelings. I both shudder and marvel now in retrospect at my own acquiescence in believing I had no power over any of it, especially myself. I had grown so accustomed to accepting how ineffectual I was, putting others' needs above my own, that I resigned myself to losing in this stepfamily game, always. As another stepmother comments,

> . . . when all efforts break down and decisions about children and who is to parent them . . . are taken to court, however powerless the biological mother may be in that . . . system, stepmothers are more so. We have no standing whatsoever. . . . Only occasionally are we considered and then it is as part of the conditions offered by the father. Does he have a good income? A good house and neighborhood for children? Is there a school close by? Does the stepmother make a good appearance on the stand?[10]

As stated previously, when you marry someone who has a child, you enter a system already set in motion, and you must conform your life around the measured establishment of theirs. At least three other people—spouse, "ex," and child, or more depending upon how many children are involved—to a large extent influence and determine your time. Having someone else decide how you spend your days brings with it a debilitating sense of lost self-control: for child, parent, *and* stepparent. It is its own unique form of stepfamily totalitarianism. The feeling of powerlessness in relation to this can be overwhelming, and how you react to this depends a great deal on how adept you are at taking care of your own needs and personal boundaries.

If you are unable to, this sense of powerlessness may find a negative vent in explosive anger, especially among stepmoms. This does not change the reality that such maternal wrath often reflects a woman raging against her own sense of impotence in the one arena where she can exert power: over her children and stepchildren. This is deadly and wrong for both mother and child. It is important at such times to focus on what I call the politics of love, the "F" world quadrupled: friendly, frank, firm, and fair.

I discovered by trial and error that stepparents must learn that they have rights and needs, too. Frequently this is difficult to remember when dealing with the imperative of "the children first." But if you cannot protect your own interests, how can you help your children and stepchildren learn to do the same for themselves? With this in mind:

Stepparenting Without Guilt Rule #12

Taking a stand as a stepparent is especially important around custody and visitation settlements because you will have to deal on a daily basis with the decision of the courts. This is not being mean but realistic, and it is important to be aware of this fact.

I'LL SEE YOU IN COURT

As with exits and reentries in scheduling, battles over children of divorce and separation form their own unique sub-category under "period of adjustment" and may dominate the new marriage for some time.[11] Do not assume that all has been worked out already between the biological parents when you marry someone with children. Even if a plan has been in effect, the remarriage itself can provoke either one or both of the parents to litigate further changes. I have worked with some children whose parents have gone to court four and five separate times over custody arguments, and with my own stepdaughter this remained one of her biggest fears. The emotional distress this creates for all, but especially for the children, is considerable, not to mention the confusion of constantly changing visitation schedules and the expense of waging legal war.

Custody battles which determine time allocation and financial support, who's with whom, where, and when frequently are a form of retaliation. One parent views remarriage as a way of getting the child(ren) back into his or her life with support from a new mate and uses the new spouse as leverage. But when men remarry and petition to change custody, it is usually the stepmothers who end up dealing with the decisions of the court. As one woman put it:

> How many men get custody of their children when they are single? So a woman marries a man expecting the typical every-other weekend visitation life but, for whatever reason, the father gets custody and the "new" wife becomes a CSM [custodial stepmother].[12]

All of a sudden, the rules change in the middle of a very convoluted game, and the custodial stepmother becomes the primary caretaker. (Not CSM but what I call the 20th century stepfamily version of PMS: provoking mothers-in-step.) Legally you and your stepchild are considered strangers; in some cases the court may decide in the stepparent's favor but only as it pertains to the "best interests and welfare of the child," *not* the stepparent or biological children from the remarriage. How many individuals in stepfamily situations learn to hate those infamous words: *for the child's own good*— as if no one else's good mattered? As another stepmother declares,

> My life rotated around [my husband's children], always what was best for the children. How can you argue against that moral argument? But I resented it a lot.[13]

So did I. And so may a number of stepparents.

In my work with blended families, I have discovered this is how two of the most painful of stepfamily emotions, resentment and guilt, find fertile ground. Resentment because of all the hard work that is involved, then guilt over feeling the resentment. (I suppose this points to the truism about hindsight being glorious, the only problem is that life must be lived moving forward, not looking back after the fact.) Ultimately I believe we do the best that we can at the time with the relational skills we have. Part of the job of being in a stepfamily is learning to use more effective interpersonal tools.

Courts base their decision upon the belief that, except in extreme cases, children have the need and right to be with two parents equally. Indeed, most children experience a deep longing to have biological ties and that special bonding with both parents. Sometimes this is where a stepparent can help bridge the gap between warring former partners because the latter can be blinded by the heat of battle and hurt pride. In my own case, there were times when I actively defended Nikki's right to be with her mother against my husband's wishes. Admittedly, a part of this was self-serving as it brought some relief for me. But it also was true that my stepdaughter sincerely wanted to be with her mom even though her father wasn't pleased about that fact.

This leads me to an extremely important point: Just because your spouse acts in incomprehensible ways when dealing with his or her children and "ex" does not mean that you have to as well. As a stepparent you actually have the opportunity to bring some level-headedness and mediation skills to the scene. One of my successes in this regard was managing phone calls between Nikki's parents. At the beginning, they were too angry and hurt with one another to communicate effectively, and this was one area where I, as the grown-up with the least emotional baggage, could help deescalate the reactivity between the two homes.

IN THE CHILD'S BEST INTERESTS

The judicial system, as I said, looks to serve the child's "best interests," but unfortunately this does not always work out in reality. When you are the object of a custody suit, you have few, if any, rights. The child or children of separation and divorce sadly often become the ammunition for getting back at ex-partners, and a lot of confrontation and struggle can go on. In my work I listen to many young people whose only wish is for their parents to stop fighting and learn how to talk to each other. I have seen a number of children who are clinically depressed over this issue. They can even accept the fact of the divorce if the animosity would only stop.

In the case of stepfamily life, a fierce desire to conquer and vanquish in the battle of the "ex" can seriously impact the new relationship. In addition, people who remarry often experience feelings of guilt and anxiety over what they've gotten themselves into which also affects the new relationship. Many stepparents wish they had taken more of an opportunity to assess the situation beforehand, to do some sober reflection, and watch the process unfold over time. As important as it is to protect the rights of the children involved, it is also important to protect your rights as a stepparent. As much as possible, find out what you are getting yourself into beforehand. Join a future stepparents group, spend time with your soon-to-be stepchildren, meet with the divorced biological parent, talk. And after remarriage if legal actions arise, find out what your options are there, too.

Many spouses may come first in their second marriage; there are those who will not due to all the needs, logistics, and possible legal maneuverings of their new partner. If the latter is the case, this is a potential breeding ground for feelings of jealousy, hurt, and anger. If the individuals involved are committed to making their relationship work, they may be able to overlook being left on the sidelines as their new spouse deals with his or her children and "ex." This is extremely important for fledgling stepparents to bear in mind because it is frightening how easily we can get sucked up into the preexisting system. What you may be expected to deal with in terms of unresolved legal issues, guilt, bitterness, disappointment, and contesting egos can be substantial. And though we all may look like adults in these trying situations, many, if not most of us, will revert to more primitive levels of behavior because we are angry and scared and feel unable to cope with the pressing demands of the new way of life we find ourselves in.

Individuals who have not had a stepfamily experience tend to underestimate the problems they will face, moving as it does in convoluted and octopus-like ways. I know I did. As stated previously, the average period of adjustment for most stepfamilies is five years. Five years of patience, compromise, communication, and tolerance are not the kind of things most people in our society are prepared to expend when we say "I do" a second time. All this warrants careful consideration beforehand.

WHO'S TO BLAME?

In my own case, I knew I did not want to experience failure again, or the likelihood of serialized relationships, even though I entertained not infrequently the divorce fantasy. You come to realize the second time around that relationships are, among other things, a commitment to work, especially on the hard stuff. I discovered a fierce tenacity around trying because I witnessed so clearly through my stepdaughter the type of disruption that can be set loose when couples disintegrate and split apart. This is not to say that leaving may not be the best course of action for all concerned; it does, however, recognize the fact that that choice comes at a price, especially for the children involved.

I have no doubt that many extended stepfamilies have battle scars and blood-curdling stories about their coming together. There may even be a tendency to play a masochistic *Can You Top This For Stepfamily Craziness?* game. It goes something like this:

The child blames the biological parent for remarrying and leaving the other parent behind; the child blames him or herself for the breakup of the marriage; the child often blames the stepparent for coming onto the scene; the spouses blame each other for just about everything; and the stepparent blames the new spouse and/or stepchild for bringing the whole mess into the new relationship in the first place. The problem with blaming others, the outside world, or ourselves is that we relinquish personal power and authority to effect change in our lives. Instead we create unhappiness or perpetuate a negative image of being unworthy of something better. This, in turn, further inhibits our ability to work toward useful solutions and creates a vicious, debilitating cycle. I had to learn this the hard way, so keep in mind:

Stepparenting Without Guilt Rule #13

Playing the "Who's-to-Blame?" Game is a no-win situation for all concerned. It only serves to fuel further antagonism between stepfamily members rather than mutuality and compromise. It is not a question of who is to blame but how you and your stepfamily go about accepting personal responsibility.

Along with blame, pity can be another lethal emotion for the individuals involved in stepfamily life as it victimizes and minimizes the various members no end. The subtle trap of feeling sorry for someone, as with blaming others, is that it relieves both them and you of personal responsibility to work on the relationship. Stepchildren do not need another grownup feeling sorry for them; they need someone to become sincerely *engaged*. Pitying others or fault finding and pointing fingers of blame are exercises in futility because ultimately one still has to deal with the reality of things as they are.

NEGOTIATING WITH THE EX

As you are working through your period of adjustment, you need to get down to the nuts and bolts of dealing with your spouse's "ex" and he or she with you. There is still the business of co-parenting (or group parenting) your stepchild. A meeting between all the adults prior to remarriage, or shortly thereafter, is an important step toward more smoothly running step relations. And if physical contact isn't possible, there is always the telephone.

I speak from personal experience here. For the first year or so after I remarried, I never spoke to Nikki's mother or laid eyes on her, although her presence was strongly felt, as I am sure mine was with her as well. At the time I always thought if the situation had been reversed I would have wanted to know about this "other woman" who was going to be a part of my child's life. Our stepfamily relations and period of adjustment progressed to the point where the two mothers, biological and step, met face to face. Looking back upon our evolution as an extended family, I think this was one of our biggest mistakes. It would have helped everybody concerned if we had all gathered together sooner and more frequently.

The reality of the stepfamily situation requires that the new spouse, whether male or female, form a relationship with the former partner in order to co-parent the children. This can be hard and nerve-wracking on both the "old" parent and "new" stepparent. When Nikki's mother and I finally did meet, I realized she was as unsure of herself and her new role as I was, which made me feel better. And I think she too was genuinely relieved to see I wasn't the wicked stepmom of fairy tale lore. At least we broke the ice; it was a start.

I believe many people who find themselves in step-relationships ask themselves similar questions: What do you do when you suddenly are thrust into intimacy with someone whom you never would have met or had anything to do with under other circumstances? It is a strange form of kinship, one that has been referred to as "wives-in-law" or "pseudo-kin."[14] The bonds and ties of stepfamily life web outward in strange and subtle ways and require that we break down the boundaries of personal interactions to include more and more people. For many this is a challenging task.

In my counseling I have heard stories of former husbands, wives, and ex-lovers stirring up feelings of rejection, jealousy, and fear. Extreme forms of this can include shouting, manipulating the children's visits, even attempts at seduction in an attempt to reestablish power.[15] If it's not illness, it's money; if it's not money, the child may be having trouble at school; if it's not that, it's something else. As one person writes,

> Both ex-husbands and ex-wives . . . exerted some influence on the reconstituted family. Usually this influence was negative. Ex-wives caused difficulty by influencing the children's attitudes toward their fathers and their father's present wives. They frequently caused jealousy on the part of the new wife. Ex-husbands aroused feelings of resentment because they either did not support the children or the payments were not regular. . . .[16]

These negative emotions can generate a continuing attachment between people who have long separated, but it is the attachment of antagonists. This can make it difficult to work out custody arrangements and the job of co-parenting on a daily basis, especially for stepparents. Be that as it may, there is still the business of raising a child and that business requires a great deal of hard-nosed emotional sobriety, setting oneself and one's own hurt, anger, pride, and neediness aside. It is tough stuff for everyone involved, especially the children, and demands a maturity many adults today cannot or will not embrace. If you are committed to working out the glitches with consistent attention, the goal of functional stepfamily relations can be achieved. The cycle of marriage, separation, divorce, and remarriage involves much more than leaving and signing documents. Several separations and divorces are required: the legal one, the emotional one, and finally a divorce from feelings of competition between the two families over the children.[17]

At the other end are partners who remain overly accommodating and considerate. This can also present problems because it points to being unable to separate emotionally from the previous relationship. For example:

> During the stage of single parenting . . . over-determined cooperation may work well. However, if a remarriage takes place and an unrecognized emotional involvement remains between ex-spouses, the new couple relationship is often strained and the lack of emotional separation from the previous spouse introduces problems.[18]

A friend of mine, divorced over ten years, admits that neither her nor her former husband's remarrying made a decided difference in their ability to co-parent. She believes having to deal with other people in the form of new spouses would have made things a lot more difficult and taxing. The ex-sleeping partner (or if you are the "ex" the new sleeping partner) becomes a ready target for upset and blame, and though not particularly helpful, it *is* human.

Jealousy and competition are emotions that are difficult and painful to experience, and many of us discover that the opportunities for these in stepfamily life are ample. There may be times when intimate moments are interrupted by a call from the ex-partner with an obligation to the past relationship which can generate feelings of hostility and hurt. Does the following sound familiar?

> Just before the newly married couple, Louise and Ralph, turn off the lights for the night, the phone rings. Ralph's ex-wife is calling to talk to him about the trouble his children have been having in school. Ralph feels guilty that he left his children behind when he divorced, and so he wishes to let his ex-wife know that he is very interested in his children. Ralph also does not want to ask his ex-wife to call at another time, because he fears she may become angry and not let his children come for their next weekend visit with him and Louise.
>
> So Ralph talks for 30 minutes to his ex-wife, while Louise lies beside him in bed, growing more and more upset. At first she says to herself, ". . . it is important for Ralph to know what is happening with his children. I have nothing to be jealous about—Ralph is married to me and he keeps telling

> me how he and his first wife couldn't get along. He loves me very much I know. . . ."
>
> Finally Louise gets up in a sudden burst of anger. . . . Anxiety crowds out [Ralph's] feelings of guilt—he feels caught somehow between two women [and] . . . draws the telephone conversation to a close. . . . Ralph and Louise each feel let down by the other, unloved and unappreciated. They had anticipated this evening would be enveloped in closeness; instead it has degenerated to bickering about Ralph and his relationship with his ex-wife.[19]

Even when all the parties involved try to do the right thing, these emotional ties from the past impact the present; this simply is part of stepfamily life. The child support payments keep going on, the telephone conversations, the meetings with counselors, back-to-school nights, switching weekends and vacation time: it is an on-going connection with the past. When dealing with former relationships, as much as humanly possible, try not to become overly involved in the problems and issues of your spouse's "ex." It is helpful to avoid knee jerk reactions and arguments you may later regret. Remember:

Stepparenting Without Guilt Rule #14

Your stepfamily situation may generate a great deal of emotional reactivity and frequently these volatile feelings are there because stepfamily members hurt in a lot of places. Often it is both useful and important to take a deep breath and count to ten before responding.

Being able to remind yourself of this beforehand is one way to navigate the tricky emotional waters and stressful situations involved in the period of adjustment of stepfamily life.

CHAPTER FOUR

A Mom Who Isn't a Mom

In the United States well over 3 million women have become stepmothers in the past five years alone, and there are about a quarter million of us new stepmoms every year.[1] This means our role in nurturing the future generations is becoming increasingly widespread and important. Mothers traditionally have carried the responsibility for the emotional life of the family, but more and more we stepmoms are taking on this role as well. A lot of it has to do with assumptions embedded deep in our history, culture, and psyche about the nature of motherhood and that the female is the bottom-line nurturer of the upcoming generations. Among the most important and lasting bonds in any human being's life are the emotions and feelings, or lack thereof, associated with the word mother, and even more today with the prefix "step." In that context, being a stepmother and stepparent can be a daunting task. As one woman cryptically states:

> As a stepmother, you are initially perceived, falsely or not, as a rival to the most traditionally revered and respected biological force in the family—Mother. If that's not enough to put some drama into your life, there's plenty more.[2]

Stepmothers are asked to perform a demanding task: to be involved and yet not too involved; to care up to a point, but not too much; to give but not to give at the same time. Are we a teacher, friend, mentor, role model, or something else entirely? According to myth we are mean, cruel, and rotten. Not only do our stepchildren hold this image of us but we and our entire culture do as well. As one stepmother writes,

> Wasn't motherhood what I said I wanted during all those years of waiting? True, I did not think of myself as the children's real mother, but I did think of myself as a "mother." It took one of my stepdaughter's small friends to tell me what I really was. I was driving the two girls home from a birthday party and was deep in my fantasy of myself as a suburban matron, chauffeuring a carload of kids, while they were silent in the back. Suddenly the friend asked, in a crystal English voice, "Is that your stepmother?" The answer came, slightly shaky, "yes." There was a pause. "Oh, I always thought a stepmother was something like a witch."[3]

We stepmothers do not want to be seen as an "evil witch," but there is a tendency to view ourselves as either good or bad with nothing in between. We stepmoms are especially prone to blame ourselves or make excuses for all the stressful feelings involved in stepfamily life. Along with our stepchildren, we feel that all the trouble is somehow our fault for not doing the right thing or not performing better on the job. According to studies we think such negative emotions as jealousy, depression, anger, and resentment are unique to us, and we do in fact experience more of these emotions than do biological mothers.[4]

As stepmothers, we often feel the need to prove ourselves as parents, especially if we have no children of our own when we remarry. Yet we often sabotage our own good intentions (a.k.a. stepparent dogooderism and superstepparenting) because children resist anyone trying to assume a biological parent's place, even if that biological parent has been less than wonderful. Indeed, our good efforts may actually make the child hurt even more when set against a backdrop of lack. The child thinks: "Why is a stranger doing more for me than my real Mom or Dad?" As one grown-up stepchild writes,

> When I look at stepfamilies in general, I am not convinced that mine turned out all that badly, though it's a situation I would not care to face again. . . . I really wouldn't want any children I might have in the future to go through this. And I cannot imagine that I would welcome being a stepparent myself. It's too problematic, too strained. Here you are an outsider trying to wedge yourself in between a parent and child—two human beings that [sic] just cannot, I believe, have a stronger bond. . . .[5]

STEPMOTHER STEREOTYPES, PITFALLS, AND MYTHS

Perhaps many stepmothers wish in retrospect that they had spent more time thinking about how all the negative images and stereotypes affected them unconsciously. Maybe it would have helped them feel less alone, "bad," and incompetent if they had been better prepared or at least forewarned. Some of the more predictable holes we stepmoms fall into include:

- unrealistic expectations about what stepfamily life is and how it works.
- a desire to make up to our stepchildren for the loss and upset caused by the death or divorce of their biological parents.
- trying to keep everybody happy and contented (a prescription for disaster).

- wanting to create a close-knit family based upon the nuclear family model.
- working too hard to disprove the wicked stepmother myth.
- the belief that we stepmoms should love our stepchildren at first sight and/or equally as our biological children.
- the expectation that our stepchildren should love us the same way they do their own parents.[6]

This leads me to an important point:

Stepparenting Without Guilt Rule #15

Avoid "should, would, could." Unless you are honest and straightforward, especially with your feelings, you won't get far in stepfamily (and family) life. Feelings are not good or bad; they simply are and need to be respected. Once they are shared honestly, the behaviors which accompany them can be worked on.

Stepmothers with no children of their own and part-time stepmoms often have the greatest trouble because they are perceived as an outsider who joins a preexisting group.[7] The ex-wife with no children who marries a man who has children does not generally have contact with her ex-husband, but her new husband maintains contact with his ex-partner. The reverse is also true: the ex-husband without children doesn't see his ex-wife but the new wife with children maintains contact with her "ex."

When two people share children, a relationship is altered but it is not closed. This can be a breeding ground for feelings of jealousy, territoriality, competition, and hurt. Again, this is not true in all stepfamily situations, but it is important to be aware that the emergence of these feelings is more likely than in intact families. Being open about the possible vulnerabilities is a must, yet it is hard to put this into practice. We live in a culture whose collective myths support tough individualism and the notion that any and all problems can be conquered with hard work and will power. Virtue and perseverance are not rewarded *ipso facto* in stepfamily life. And if they are, it may take longer to achieve them. Our society as a whole is addicted to short-term gain, but in trying to develop and establish a stepfamily, it is the long-term goal that must be the focus.

INHIBITION OF FEELINGS

Another issues we stepmothers experience which is unique is feeling the necessity of reigning in our feelings for fear of invading the "real" parent's territory. Many times this often is experienced in only a fleeting moment, when a stepparent says, "Better not get involved with that one; that's the mother's (or father's) turf." Says one stepmother:

> I really would like to fuss with [my stepdaughter] more. You know, help her pick clothes and fix her hair. But I guess I'd better not get mixed up in her mother's territory. She likes me now and will take some advice if I'm careful. I don't want to spoil anything by making waves.[8]

Sometimes we may have to restrain our feelings for no other reason than to make it through a hectic stepparenting day and the demands of stepfamily scheduling. Often our interactions with our stepchildren are interrupted because they have to go back to their other home. This is no one's fault; it is simply a reality in stepfamily life. Once again there are tiny barriers that remind us of the differences involved.

On the other hand, some stepparents go the other way and try too hard, as I did in the beginning. It is an unfulfilling cycle of frustration and non-fulfillment: the more warm and caring you are, the harder you try; the harder you try (often with little results), the more frustrated, angry, and depressed you get; then more problems can arise and the situation festers from all the negative feelings and emotions involved. So keep in mind that results put forth for effort accrue in inverse proportion to the energy you expend. Please take note of this widespread pattern of stepfamily experience.

APPROPRIATE BOUNDARIES AND LIMITS

Ambivalence is one of the primary emotional experiences of being a mother, especially of the step variety.[9] I have often asked myself as a stepparent: How long does it take to learn how to say no? To be fair to yourself and your own children? Or to your stepchild? One thing I learned is that you are much more inclined to give other people's children the benefit of the doubt than your own. This is a large trap for many stepparents, especially stepmothers. Learning how to negotiate these subtle boundaries and emotional limits is an important task.

Here is what happened to one stepmother who was unable to bear this in mind:

> I knew when I married Charles that Lena [his daughter] was a disturbed child. She always had been hyperactive and a behavior problem . . . but seeing her father and me getting along well would be one difference. So Charles and I got married and I tried and tried, and then tried harder and harder, but Lena kept right on behaving the way she always had. I sent my own daughter back to live with her father because the friction between the two girls was so horrible. But that didn't help, and I got more and more angry, and I began to hate Lena, and Charles got mad at me and we fight. . . . I don't know where to turn.[10]

This type of situation can become a downward spiral of frustration and non-fulfillment where the situation only gets worse rather than heals. By way of contrast, here is a stepmother who knew what her limits were and more importantly how to keep them:

> [My husband-to-be] wanted Janie to live with us. Her mother made no arguments, but I said no. The kid wanted to make the move and reach out for my love, but I knew what I could do and what I wasn't able to do, this was too much. I was honest with my future husband right from the start and told him I'd never want Janie to live with us. I can't handle her, she's too disturbed. Alan got mad at first, but I'd have never married him if she came along. Even now I panic on her scheduled visits.[11]

Honesty is the best policy if you know yourself well and how to listen to your own heart. I suspect that many stepmothers (and stepfathers) trying to "do the right thing" fall into the trap of not listening to their own needs. Nevertheless, setting appropriate limits is critical in stepfamily life because physical and psychological boundaries are so different. Stepfamilies come together often having incompatible world views, value systems, ways of celebrating events and holidays, attitudes about what is right, wrong, and "normal," and the settling in period, as I have said, can be trying. Firm boundaries and knowing what you can and cannot handle go a long way toward helping this situation. I encourage the following:

Stepparenting Without Guilt Rule #16

If you honestly and sincerely cannot deal with your stepchild, do not lie to yourself that you can. Accept your limitations and don't punish yourself for something you are unable to achieve. Honor what you can do and work from there.

STEPMOTHER ASSETS VS. LIABILITIES

In my own life as a stepmom, I have often wondered:

Who profits whom in all this? Is the stepmother an asset to the biological parent and because of this a liability to herself? I recall an instance once in a restaurant where I overheard a woman bragging to a friend. They were laughing and clicking glasses in a toast. "Here's to our being out! Why should I get married again? I get regular child support payments and have a built-in baby sitter on weekends" (baby sitter being synonymous with new stepmother). I could have leapt out of my seat and choked her. I felt like shouting, *"Do you know how unbelievably hard it is being a stepparent? How much work is involved?!"* I wonder how many stepmothers have experienced variations on this emotional theme?

This points to the fact that generally the stepmother's work profits the biological mother and father, possibly even the stepchild(ren), but not herself. The biological child might want to skip a scheduled visit but the biological mom or dad may be so in need of getting the child out of the house that he or she comes to rely on the stepparent for time off. Comments one stepparent,

> There's no justice. She [the biological mother] left her kids, is off traveling and working, and I get the day-to-day drudgery of raising them. Then she shows up for visits, crams them full of treats and presents, and collects the mommy goodies. After she disappears again, I get to hear how successful and wonderful she is, as well as having to live with the grief her visits stir up. I feel terribly resentful, but there's nothing I can do. There are few rewards to this job.[12]

This certainly is not true of all stepparenting situations where both biological parents share equal responsibility in raising their children. On the other hand, this does not alter the fact that many stepparents carry a large portion of the child-rearing work in remarriage. Someday, too, the children of remarriage are going to have to deal with the emotional residue of "real" mom or dad not being there while "cruel" stepmom or stepdad is left doing the nuts and bolts, hands-on job of day-to-day parenting. These are difficulties intact families do not face.

If being overly accommodating and solicitous is one of your stepparenting problems, as it was mine, I suggest being firm and realistic about what you need. After some hard knocks, I finally came to know what would tip me over the deep end, and I got to the point of being able to withstand my husband's disappointment whenever I did not go along with his wishes and dreams for his daughter. This requires what I call "dark" honesty with yourself and your spouse. It may be unpleasant to hear, but it is the truth and being truthful, I believe, is the fountainhead of all else. Having said that, it is important to bear in mind that being truthful in a mean-spirited or hostile way is not the same as sharing what is true for you with compassion. As I mentioned earlier: Stepfamily life is a journey toward emotional maturity which requires even greater efforts toward conscious, caring behavior.

CHANGING ROLES, CHANGING TIMES

So many traditional roles are changing today for everyone: men, women, children, and marriage. Some women are working while their husbands stay home; both parents may be working with or without additional help for their children; single parenting households are on the rise; some stepmoms go to work to support the children from a previous marriage while the biological mother is at home; maybe the stepmother is at home raising someone else's children while that someone is out doing something exotic and self-fulfilling.

In a very brief time span from an historical perspective we have moved from rural living to urban to suburban living with many of us moving through life in a car programmed according to a schedule to go back and forth between two or more households, children sleeping in the back seat of a car barreling down the freeways between Mom and Dad.

In the early days of our stepfamily journey, I was doing the traditional mommy things: washing clothes, combing tangled hair, reading bedtime stories (Donnica and Mousie especially), and helping Nikki pick up her toys. But I was not the Mommy, and Nikki reminded me of this constantly. I would feel anger and hurt a lot of the time, and it took me quite a while to realize this was a defense she used against missing her mom. In a cryptic comment several researchers write:

> It is interesting to speculate . . . whether changes in the attitudes and aspirations of women in recent years will have implications for their readiness to accept a position as stepmother which involve[s] fulfilling a 'traditional' maternal role toward someone else's children. [13]

Understatement indeed. It is hard for me to accept that I am not "real," flesh, blood, stepparenting foibles, and all, and other stepparents may feel the same way. Stepparenting and stepfamily life in particular can involve a lot of sharp edges, bumps, scratches, and cracks; they certainly are not for those who must be carefully kept. As stepparents we often have responsibility without authority which can be painful and feel very disempowering at times. As one stepmother says,

> . . . on several occasions a phone call from Dave's former wife would bring in its wake the unexpected arrival, for the next six months to a year, of two children and a dog into living spaces designed for two people. With their presence came responsibility but little power, a dynamic that debilitates in any situation.[14]

Another stepmom declares that her mate would not consider having more children of their own because of the financial commitments to his first set of biological off-spring, her stepchildren:

> The pain of the bonds of my stepfamily go deeper than money. . . I wanted to have more than one child. Largely because of the time, energy, financial commitment, and ongoing responsibility that [my husband] has expended over the years for [his two children], he is unwilling to consider a second child of our own. For me this painful price of living in a stepfamily is ever-present.[15]

One can see the deep effect of step life on this particular stepmother. Furthermore, sometimes the stepparent's own biological children receive less attention as he or she has to deal with the children of a former marriage. This can create quite a dilemma: On the one hand, you bear witness to the pain and suffering of individuals who come into your life unexpectedly and without much choice; on the other, you experience compassion for yourself for being caught in the middle and the instinctual concern of a parent to protect your own off-spring. As one individual writes,

> One of the saddest laments of stepmothers who have children of their own is about sharing the energy and time they once devoted to their own children. They feel torn, and in trying to be good stepmothers, many discover they slight their own children.[16]

This, too, was my experience. In the early stages of our period of adjustment I know our first child was deprived of a great deal of my attention due to the overwhelming demands of having to deal with my stepdaughter. I carried around a large amount of personal guilt over this issue, and as the years went by I consciously tried to give back to my son what I know he missed during the beginning years of my remarriage. So remember:

Stepparenting Without Guilt Rule #17

There is a point where your biological children come first, and this has nothing to do with being mean or wicked. You do not have to save your stepchildren at the expense of your own off-spring. Being firm and realistic about their needs will help you be a better stepparent as well.

CONFLICTING LOYALTIES

One of the problems you may face as a stepparent is that of divided loyalties and how to modulate conflicting interactions between various stepfamily members and half-siblings. If someone has several children and one in particular has a problem, the parents and others may not be thrilled about the situation, but the biological ties bind them and they try to hold on. These deep connections *create* a reason for holding on. Yet even intact families can break down under the stress of certain life situations, and in stepfamilies these dynamics can become infinitely more problematic and tricky. In stepfamily life, the ramifications and repercussions can go on and on.

I would like other stepparents, especially women, who are considering remarriage with children to ask themselves sincerely:

- Am I capable of handling this?
- Can I truly be there for a child who is in the deepest sense not my own?
- Can I be honest about all my feelings, especially the ambivalent ones?

I want men and women who already have children and who are contemplating remarriage to consider what they are asking of their off-spring and future spouse:

- How is it possible to be fair to all concerned?
- How much can you ask your child or your new mate to accommodate?
- Where do you draw the line between whose rights and needs should prevail at any given time?
- Where will the new marriage relationship stand within in all these convoluted boundaries?

These are difficult questions both to ask and to answer but important ones to address nevertheless, especially around the issue of conflicting loyalties. Stepparents, and especially stepmothers, both present and future, would do well to consider them prior to saying "I do."

CHAPTER FIVE

Emotional Minefields of Stepfamily Life

In medieval literature, the Seven Deadly Sins represented spiritual minefields of anger, covetousness, envy, gluttony, sloth, lust, and pride (considered by St. Thomas Aquinas the worst of all). I have come to believe that stepfamily life has its own unique panoply of emotional challenges, all of which can be toxic if left unacknowledged and unexplored as they arise along the way. A few that come to mind include:

- fear
- anxiety
- guilt
- anger
- jealousy
- resentment
- betrayal
- abandonment
- hurt
- low self esteem
- stress
- grief and loss

Most, if not all, stepfamilies have difficult emotions to work through. We stepparents may walk into contentious circumstances overnight, and it can be a real eye-opener for those of us who are unsuspecting or unprepared. We may find ourselves functioning in a climate of anger, fatigue, and manipulation where painful emotions come rapidly to the center of our lives. This can be doubly and triply hard for those who haven't learned how to deal with painful emotions from their own families of origin—which, in all likelihood, is most of us.

As much upheaval as biological parents experience having children, I believe remarried couples with children experience more. Interviews with remarried families reveal a decided *lack* of positive emotions, as well as considerable negative feelings, toward this new way of life.[1] Writes one authority,

> . . . even previously relaxed parents may become troubled stepparents or partners of stepparents and many comfortable and well behaved children may become upset and disagreeable stepchildren. It is apparent that stepfamily culture . . . can produce stressful life situations and consequent emotional conflicts in individuals who have coped and can cope successfully with other aspects of their lives.[2]

Many professionally trained psychologists admit that their therapeutic and counseling skills have not prepared them for the hardships of being a stepparent and living in a stepfamily when they experienced them first-hand.[3] It is amazing how clinical insight and expertise can fly out the window when stepfamily emotions boil and flare.

DEFENSE MECHANISMS

Before looking at some of the more prevalent feelings in stepfamily life, a few words about how we cope with difficult emotional material may be useful. When we are unprepared for something, the basic psychological defense mechanism for most of us is denial. Denial is fairly straightforward: we simply disavow the existence of something. Anger? Guilt? Resentment? Who, me? Denial is our refusal to accept a reality that feels threatening. The bad stuff simply is not there, end of story.

Repression is another defense mechanism whereby we block feelings that disturb us by pushing them out of our awareness. If repression is excessive, these impulses find expression in neurotic and other dysfunctional physical, behavioral, and/or psychological symptoms. With repression, the adage is out of sight, out of mind.

Rationalization is another frequently employed defensive technique. By using this we talk ourselves out of anxiety-provoking experiences by making the unacceptable appear acceptable. We convince ourselves that the situation we are in isn't really all *that* bad and we carry on. It is one way of dealing with the unique unhappiness and pain we may be confronting in stepfamily life.

Along with denial, repression, and rationalization, there are two other defense mechanisms known as projection and displacement. While the first three take place intrapsychically, i.e. within the mind of the individual, the latter two do not. Projection and displacement are interpsychic in that they involve another person in the mental/emotional feedback loop.

Displacement puts the negative emotion that we are feeling onto another person. It transfers difficult material from its source (for instance, the parent) onto a more acceptable one (for example, the stepparent). Displacement is an effective defense mechanism because it is less threatening to be angry with someone else other than yourself or an important primary relational bond.[4] For example:

> Much of the misplaced anger so common to step is based on the original breakup and the grievances and distortions surrounding that. A stepchild often unconsciously feels that he has to punish a stepparent—it's a way of getting even with the real parent. . . .[5]

The stepparent may bear the brunt of the displaced hostile feelings within the stepfamily; and needless to say, this is not an enviable position to hold. The child may not actively hate you as a stepmom or stepdad, but you become the easiest target for all the hurt feelings. One woman reports it took five years for her to get to the truth surrounding the trouble she was experiencing with her stepdaughters: they still were angry with their father for leaving their biological mother. The stepdaughters had nothing against their stepmother per se; she merely was the one to receive all the flack.[6] As understandable as this may be from the child's point of view, it makes it difficult for us stepparents to like our new stepchildren. It is also important to point out that displacement is an equal opportunity defense mechanism: the child often becomes an easy target for our negative feelings as stepparents. If you are angry at your new spouse for lack of support, you may take it out on your stepchildren (as well as on the ex-spouse, your own kids, and/or yourself).

Projection, though similar to displacement in that it involves another person, functions somewhat differently. With projection the individual attributes his or her negative feelings or wishes to someone else because he cannot take the responsibility for them him/herself.[7] The stepparent who hates his or her stepchild believes the child carries that negative emotion. The stepchild who resents his or her stepparent believes the stepparent carries the feeling. This allows the person doing the projecting to maintain a more positive self-image.

There are other defense mechanisms in our emotional repertoire but denial, repression, rationalization, displacement, and projection are among the most common. Working on recognizing and embracing these defensive patterns is critical, for without taking personal responsibility, nothing can be done to move the stepfamily situation in a more positive direction. Saying this is easy; doing it, however, can be hard as primal emotions such as jealousy, anger, and fear erupt.

FEAR AND ANXIETY

Fear and anxiety are at the bedrock of most of our difficult emotional experiences and the coping mechanisms we put in place to defend against them. Fear and anxiety that are examined can be helpful because they lead to some form of solution making process which in turn can alleviate stress. When unexamined, however, these emotions may become toxic because they form a continuous negative feedback loop which only compounds stepfamily problems. The more we try to ignore anxiety and fear, the more they grow in power and strength. The more we repress, deny, rationalize, displace, and/or project these emotions, the more they fester and abscess.

Children especially show fears around the fact that they have experienced the loss of a parent, the dissolution of their original family, and the understandable anxiety that this could happen again. These emotions frequently arise from the sense of insecurity, the lack of belongingness, and role confusion which often are characteristic of stepfamily life. The uncomfortable feelings that can be aroused in us from threats to our security are potentially many in stepfamily life and require careful and consistent diffusing.

Stepparenting Without Guilt Rule #18
Happiness and trust cannot be achieved when fear and anxiety are at their base. This applies to all members of the stepfamily, adult and child alike. Learning how to view fear and anxiety as signposts which can direct us toward new and positive ways of interacting is important in stepfamily life.

GUILT

As mentioned previously, guilt is among the most frequently experienced stepfamily emotion. There are two basic kinds of guilt: real and imagined. Real or genuine guilt occurs when an individual does not fulfill an obligation or commitment to another person which is reasonable to expect.[8] It is not manipulative but rather task-specific. If we promise to do something which is within our ability to do and then do not perform, it is appropriate that we experience some guilt for breaking our word or commitment. Real guilt encourages us to take stock of our actions and needs to be addressed in an honest, straightforward way.

Guilt that is not situation or task specific generally is imaginary guilt. Imaginary guilt puts us in a pattern of self-accusation and blame which in turn prevents us from confronting deeper issues. Imaginary guilt occurs when we believe we are responsible for other people's actions when we, in fact, are not or that our worth is based on how others perceive us and our behavior.[9] It can cause problems and a sense of personal failure in any family but in stepfamilies especially. I experienced guilt from carrying around so many angry feelings a lot of the time. I know Nikki experienced guilt because she felt that "all the trouble" was somehow her fault.

But in stepfamily life, you often marry into a lot of guilt. Each member of the stepfamily can carry his or her own variation on this theme: guilt felt by the parent or child for being the cause of the breakup; guilt for not being able to love your stepparent or your stepchild; guilt over the resentment you feel for having to deal with your partner's "ex"; guilt over hating the many unexpected demands inherent in the whole situation. As one veteran stepparent writes,

> The guilt, the anxiety, and the mixture of parental feelings stirred up by separation from some of one's children before they are grown, combined with the guilt, the anxiety, and the mixture of parental feelings of one's spouse, who may be in a similar situation, hardly make for a household characterized by serenity and soft music.[10]

As I said earlier: more sour notes at first that not. Guilt is often the primary emotion for stepmothers especially. Here are a just few possibilities:

- Guilt for not loving our stepchildren.
- Guilt because we are not selfless.
- Guilt over feeling powerless to do anything about it except leave (divorce fantasy).
- Guilt from high expectations which are unattainable and disappointment when these expectations are not achieved.
- Guilt from a sense of inadequacy in coping with all the new demands.
- Guilt over being flawed and imperfect and having awful fantasies about everybody—spouse, stepchild, *and* "ex."
- Guilt over succumbing to the wicked stepparent myth.[11]

There are numerous ways this guilt can manifest itself. In my own case, I went through all the variations: If you do not love your stepchild(ren), you feel guilty. If you care for them a lot, you feel guilty because you know that you should not try to replace the biological parent. If you do not want your stepchildren around, you feel guilty. If you argue with your new spouse about your stepchildren, you feel guilty. And when he or she accuses you of being jealous, you feel guiltier still because it may be true and as the grown up you're not supposed to feel that way, right? Plus, you have to deal with your spouse's guilt for putting his/her children and you in this predicament in the first place.

My inability at times to respond sincerely "I love you" to Nikki's constant "Do you love me?" made me feel guilty and only served to confirm my imagined stepmotherly nastiness most of the time. In retrospect I don't know why I automatically assumed I should or could fulfill her need and hunger for love, but I did. This is important to bear in mind because feeling guilty about not loving your stepchildren can be rough. Just remember that you do not need to feel love at first in order to make your stepfamily situation work. Remind yourself that love is the product of the process itself, the fruit of all the hard work and because of this is far sweeter once it is finally achieved.

Fathers and stepfathers are not exempt from feelings of guilt either. Men who leave children behind experience guilt and often overcompensate for this by giving time and money to the children from their former relationship. This is one of the issues my husband and I grappled with in the early stages of our period of adjustment. Or the father can provide for the new family at the expense of the old one and feel guilty about that, too. Sometimes the guilt is so great, the father simply disappears because the pain is too much to bear. He may drop out of his children's lives altogether because it is too difficult to see them only occasionally. One father/stepfather describes his feelings:

> There is a tremendous amount of guilt. . . . I think that maybe I was naive, but I had hoped that in some ways,

> though I felt I could never make up to my natural children for leaving, that I would be able to provide a substitute experience for them with me and with my new family that would at least partially compensate for the fact that I wasn't there in the old [one]. . . .[12]

Stepparents and parents need to be prepared to confront a sense of guilt in their relationships and the triangles which are likely to occur because of this in stepfamily life. Guilt arises when family members feel they cannot meet the challenges of their new experience. We stepparents often feel guilty and to blame when our stepchildren act out rather than seeing their behavior as stemming from their own frustrated feelings and needs. In stepfamily life it is important that each member has the right to make his or her own mistakes and be held accountable for individual behavior. This applies to both biological and stepchildren and can help keep the guilt factor in check.

Children also experience guilt and ambivalence, though many may be unable to express it verbally. They may feel guilty about the break-up of their parents' marriage, wondering if they caused the divorce. I believe Nikki felt guilty that her parents were so angry with one another, as if she somehow were responsible for their emotional response, and this is a terrific burden for a child to bear. In addition, with the capacity for magical thinking where children experience themselves as omnipotent, they may wish for the mother or father to die, go away, or simply disappear. When this happens in divorce, children can often feel guilty and at the same time powerful. If children believe that their angry wishes or unruly behavior caused the original break up, they may feel anxious and guilty whenever they experience tension between the new couple. [13] They may even feel guilty about liking their new stepparent as if this somehow threatens the biological relationship, making them disloyal to that bond. A biological father comments:

> My younger girl has some problems because her real mother keeps calling her up and promising her monetary things if she will come and live with her and all the girl really wants is affection, which my [second] wife gives. So the child is torn between two poles at this point. I think she feels guilty for loving [her stepmother] as much, if not more, than her real mom.[14]

All this only compounds the pattern of stepfamily guilt. One boy expresses the conflicting emotions well:

> The culture shock coming to visit [non-custodial parent] is bad. I have to get used to new rules. Everything is different and I feel strange.[15]

ANGER

Anger is another primary emotion in stepfamily life. When you remarry someone with children, do not be surprised if you step into a hotbed of volatile and hostile feelings right away. How much anger can there be? Sometimes a lot, and most frequently it is your own.

- Anger with the child (stepchild) for not adjusting to the new family.
- Anger from the child directed toward the biological parent for leaving and upsetting the original family unit.
- Anger with the stepparent for interrupting the relationship the child had with his or her single parent.
- Anger at the stepparent for preventing the fantasy reunion between the biological parents.
- Anger with the spouse for including his/her children as part of the deal.
- Anger with the "ex" simply for being there.
- Anger for all the trouble.[16]

There can be so much anger in stepfamilies it may feel overwhelming at times, especially if you grew up in a family where getting angry was considered unacceptable behavior, which is true for many of us. What follows is from a successful journalist who nevertheless was baffled by her role as a stepparent and the anger she experienced in this role:

> For the first time in my life I was tongue-tied. Disbelieving what was going on, I sat stymied, too afraid to speak. Should I let that anger out, it would surely disembowel our new marriage. . . . Once . . . I attempted to talk with my husband about it. I struck out. I got nowhere in the battle of my-children, your-children. They were no problem, he said.—*I* was the problem. For the first time in my adult life I felt helpless. What had I gotten myself into? I'd rather interview the President, cover a plane crash, have 17 for dinner than spend those lonely days trying to figure out how I could manage this job of mother, stepmother, wife. . . .[17]

Competence in one area of life does not necessarily translate into the stepfamily arena, and a great deal of the time we can feel overwhelmed and angry without any specific answers how to make the situation better. Along with these feelings of anger is an accompanying sense of isolation and being unable to express ourselves, like the woman above. What we future stepparents fail to appreciate before entering remarriage with children is how strongly these emotions can influence our new life. And the more people who are involved in the stepfamily equation, the more potential for trauma, anger, and heartache. It is vital to acknowledge this from the start and to continue to do so as time goes on because being in a stepfamily requires maintaining a fair amount of focused emotional presence. As indicated earlier, the goal of success in this type of family structure is long range.

Having said that, it is still possible even after years for this darker side to reemerge and churn up angry feelings which we believe were long buried. Because in many cases, time does not necessarily heal. Or it can require much more patience to make inroads into that healing. Old animosities can resurface in a twinkling, and we may be back to square one, especially as stressful developmental stages are reached. In stepfamily life, trying to deal with the weight of all the things left unsaid, and the space and silence between the words that are is a task which requires ongoing commitment and practice. So remember:

Stepparenting Without Guilt Rule #19

Do not talk ill of the absent parent or other stepfamily members. Mean-spirited comments only come back to haunt you and reinforce the evil stepparent myth. While it is important to acknowledge anger, you also have a choice how to express it; sometimes prudent detachment is the best policy.

JEALOUSY

Jealousy is another provocative force in stepfamilies. We may find ourselves in a climate of jealousy and manipulation which demands large reserves of forbearance, understanding, and humor—precious commodities seldom in abundant supply when stressful and difficult situations present themselves and we feel taxed and stretched to our limits already. When these reserves run dry or are not there in the first place, there can be trouble. As two biological parents comment:

> I think my [second] husband was jealous of my daughter from the day we got married. She now lives with her dad because she was a nervous wreck.[18]

> The twins and my stepdaughter hate each other. The rest of the kids get along all right, but I don't think there's a great deal of love there. They always pull this bit about "your mommie" and "my daddy" jazz. There's lots of jealousy

> among them. The kids drive us crazy with fighting. I think it has gotten worse.[19]

Not only can there be jealousy and in-fighting between stepparents and stepchildren, step and half-siblings but also between the various adults involved as well: jealousy of the time spent dealing with the past; jealousy over the ex-partner (or current partner if you are the "ex"); jealousy over all the attention that gets focused elsewhere. Jealousy is one of the most difficult emotions to admit to and own because while we may not like feeling angry, guilty, fearful, or anxious, they somehow appear more acceptable than jealousy. If you are jealous, you must not be a very understanding or forgiving person. In stepfamily life, however, if jealousy is there, it must be addressed and worked on. If left unacknowledged, this is what can happen:

> I experience a complex emotional package of jealousy, anger, and fear. I am jealous of his ex-wife. I am jealous of his children, especially his two daughters. I feel inadequate; I feel paralyzed . . . inarticulate, scared. . . .[20]

A number of individuals involved in stepfamily life may experience similar emotional reactions.

RESENTMENT

Resentment may be one of the most debilitating emotions experienced in stepfamilies. Resentment finds fertile soil in our lives when we feel we are being forced into something which we do not want or over which we feel we have little or no control, and there are numerous opportunities for this in stepfamily life.[21] This applies equally to a stepparent who feels forced to love and deal with a stepchild or a stepchild who has to cope with a new stepparent and family. What better way to create resentment than to make an individual feel he or she must choose or do something he/she does not want? As one person comments,

> As cold as this may sound, I know of several stepmothers who, by insisting that they love the stepchild just like their own, create a situation where resentments are expressed in unconscious and unintended ways and where children feel confused and manipulated by the discrepancy between what they are told and what they experience.[22]

Resentment, along with jealousy, is potentially one of the more destructive stepfamily emotions; it is a tough one to admit to and own. While jealousy was not predominant, I certainly harbored a great deal of resentment during the early stages of my remarriage and have some sense of what this emotion can do both psychologically and physically. The resentment I experienced during our early stepfamily years felt far too powerful and destructive to express. Like the journalist quoted earlier, I believed it would ruin my marriage if let out, so I kept it inside. In my case it went deep down, literally wrapping itself around my heart. I handled resentment so well—or rather poorly—that it festered into cancer by my mid-thirties. Stepfamily life was by no means the singular cause of my illness. But pre-existing emotional patterns which I brought into my marriage and which were maladaptive to begin with became infinitely worse under the stress and demands of stepfamily life.

It all becomes so convoluted internally:

If you cannot express anger, you feel resentment and then guilt over that resentment because it is difficult not to feel and act guilty when resentment is underneath. Feelings of anger and helplessness also breed resentment which can then be followed by more anger and guilt again. It becomes a vicious, insidious cycle. You can know this rationally, understand it rationally, and still resent the situation you find yourself in. This applies to all members of your stepfamily, especially the children who may resent the remarriage. For me, it took a life-threatening illness to *finally* become starkly honest about these feelings. It was a high price to pay, but once the honesty was in place, things started slowly to improve. If you cannot get that dark honesty out, it has nowhere else to go but implode inwards.

LOW SELF-ESTEEM

Another issue that arises in stepfamily life with greater frequency than intact families is low self-esteem.[23] Children of broken relationships often rationalize "I must not be that important or loved if Mommy and Daddy left." Or, "If I had been good enough, maybe Mom and Dad would still be together." In stepfamily life, for the children and new spouse especially, there is a sense of having to live with the consequences of other people's actions, decisions, and choices. This situation—responsibility without power—generates feelings of low self-esteem and lack of personal worth which in turn can lead to depression.[24] Children are expected by the biological parent who has remarried to be happy. And the new stepparent may expect this also, both of the children involved and of him or herself. But in stepfamilies, as in life generally, our expectations frequently do not unfold as we imagine or would always like. The numerous challenges you may have to deal with in stepfamily life can make you feel unsure of yourself. And the sense of being isolated and alone does not help improve self-image either.

For children, remarriage can also affect their sense of trust and personal value. On some level, they may fear that all relationships are doomed to failure, and they can carry with them a sense of impending doom ("What's going to happen next?"). The new stepparent may leave as did the biological one, and some children believe that they will be rejected again. Statistics on the high failure rate of remarriage support this view.

Another problem in this particular situation is that the stepchild does not have a real claim on his or her stepparent's affection. Biological children assume this affection, but stepchildren cannot. In remarriage, the children may be scared, cautious, jealous, timid, angry, withdrawn, or various combinations of all these emotions. Or they can be bounced back and forth so much that they lose a sense of themselves altogether, which can further reinforce a negative self-image. Indeed, such youngsters even come to look upon "not being okay" as a part of their lives. After one particularly challenging weekend, Nikki turned to me and asked: "Why can't I be a regular kid in one place with my own life? How come I have to do all this?" It was one of the most painful things I heard ever her say. Why, indeed, couldn't she be "just a kid"?

STRESS

Stress is ever present for all of us today, but in steplife it is hard to imagine how stressful and stress-filled it can be. As mentioned, emotional patterns and personal interactions in stepfamilies are far more intricate than in intact families due to numbers and logistics, and this in itself is very stress-provoking.[25] At the risk of sounding simplistic, I wish someone had told me this before I remarried. At the time it felt as if I had been dropped into a jungle or foreign country without knowing the language or having the requisite survival tools. I clearly was left to fend for myself in uncharted territory. During the first three years of my remarriage, I remember spending a lot of time simply feeling numb. I am sure there are other stepparents who have experienced similar stress reactions.

The *Diagnostic and Statistical Manuel of Mental Disorders* cites Post-traumatic Stress Disorder (PTSD) among its anxiety disorders and lists "sudden destruction of one's home or community" among the precipitating factors. Bad dreams, psychological and emotional numbing; disruption of normal sleeping patterns; restricted range of affect (i.e. unable to have loving feelings); hyper-vigilance, outbursts of irritability and anger; exaggerated startle response; withdrawal and listlessness are among the criteria listed to diagnose this disorder.[26] This has a number of applications to stepfamily life, and I see variations of this type of reaction among more than a few individuals who are in stepfamilies, both young and old. All the people and maneuvering involved, along with having to address perplexing situations and painful emotions, generate a kind of stress peculiar to this way of life.

Unfortunately, we often deny or rationalize the stress away once our stepchild is gone or we have hung up the phone with an ex-partner. Our stepchildren may do the same thing after waving good-bye. As frequently is the case with most defense mechanisms, this is another form of self-deception because relief from stress often makes it appear less real. In reality, however, it is simply another way we deny the truth of what is going on. Awareness of the impact of cumulative stress and ways of alleviating it are critical to stepfamily survival. Chronic stress can have decidedly negative consequences on both our mental and physical well being. If the body—whether physical, emotional, *or* marital—absorbs too much, the consequences can be dire. I speak from personal experience in this regard.

GRIEF AND LOSS

In the final analysis, perhaps the biggest factor influencing the reformed stepfamily is how the various members deal with loss, along with the accompanying feelings of abandonment, betrayal, and grief. This cannot be emphasized enough because at the bottom of the emotional wells of anger, jealousy, resentment, and guilt is sadness over what is gone. Fundamentally important relationships have been disrupted, and this is one of the most difficult readjustments many members of stepfamilies have to make. It is also something which cannot be forced because the wounds of a marriage or relationship breaking apart can take a long time to heal, especially for the children involved. Grown-ups lose a marriage and their ideal of romance and youth; children lose a parent and their home, their sense of security and belonging; and a stepparent who has never been married before loses the chance of sharing first love and birth.

This loss can be imprinted for a long time, perhaps years, and these scars may be slow to mend, especially with children, because their feelings of vulnerability can far outlast those of adults. Adults may be quite happy in their new life, single or remarried, while the children grieve and must deal with feelings of confusion, hurt, and divided loyalties. What is seen as a gain to the adult (single life or remarriage) often is viewed as a loss to the child (Mommy and Daddy will not get back together again). For the children especially, life has not worked out as planned. As Nikki so poignantly stated: it is hard for a child to understand the complexities of love dying. One person writes,

> Stepfamily members have a lot of sore spots. They're angry at everyone including themselves for what has happened. Parents snap at their children. Kids fight among themselves or with adults. Stepparents get their feelings hurt and shout or pout. Everyone has a chip on his or her shoulder, and there are plenty of people around to knock it off.[27]

What some stepfamilies experience in the way of emotional difficulties may not apply to others, but this is the way we were. It is also important to remember that each of us deals with loss differently. Some of us may become emotional; others defensive and reactive; some quietly restrained; while still others opt for loudness, drama, and flamboyance. In addition, psychological factors, cultural expectations, and our own personal life experiences all contribute to how we respond to loss, and the way we approach this issue can impact the second relationship for years. [28]

The sad truth is that in many cases stepfamily life is founded as much upon loss, separation, and heartache, along with feelings of betrayal and abandonment, as it is upon feelings of hopefulness and renewal. There can be confusion, competitiveness, and hurt which must be addressed if there is to be hope for the second marriage and stepparenting to succeed. And very few individuals enter a new relationship thinking how sad, difficult, and stress-provoking it is going to be. It feels unnatural, perverse almost, to be so negative about the future. But contemplating remarriage with children requires that you keep this in mind because all the pain can make everybody feel mildly upset to thoroughly miserable. More pain comes from the simple fact that there are more people involved, more needs to be met, and more loss to deal with. This sensitivity and defensiveness around feelings of abandonment can make stepfamily relationships turbulent for years.

In her work on death and dying, Elisabeth Kübler-Ross suggests the following five stages to be worked through in the grieving process:

- denial
- anger
- bargaining
- depression
- acceptance[29]

Most stepfamilies need to engage in a similar grieving process which parallels in many ways the period of adjustment phases of disillusionment, crises, reevaluation, and acceptance. One of the ways we dealt with these painful emotions was during regular meetings called Family Council which I will discuss in the next chapter. The important point to remember is that at the bedrock of all the negative emotions in stepfamily life are feelings of grief and sadness over what has been lost and will not be regained. These feelings must be confronted in the formation of blended families if there is hope for their future success. Remember:

Stepparenting Without Guilt Rule #20

Stepfamilies are born of loss. Accept and honor this fact and the heartache which accompanies it. With work and persistence, belief in the new stepfamily can arise.

CHAPTER SIX

Council and Communication

WHEN MELISSA, our youngest child, was three years old and Nikki almost eleven we began an activity which we have continued on and off ever since: Family Council.[1] Our version of Family Council involves semi-regular gatherings where various members can air their views (or vent their spleen as the case may be) and where listening is deemed as important, if not more so, as talking. It has been one of the ways we have built a blended family tradition working as a stepfamily unit.

In Council, we practice expressing our feelings in a noncritical way, and it functions as an ongoing forum where all sides can be heard. Often this can be difficult as most of us tend to become emotionally reactive, volatile, and defensive when tender emotions are involved. Notice I say difficult, but not impossible. Giving undivided attention, encouraging conversation, asking questions, sorting out the overt and covert messages, taking responsibility for our own actions and feelings along with showing genuine empathy: these are all aspects of Council we work on. Once hurtful and painful feelings are identified and expressed, there is the possibility for more positive ones to emerge. We have learned over the years of council practice that trust has the opportunity of growing where honesty is present. Sometimes that honesty can be hard to hear and embrace, but it has been my experience that it helps us forward as a family.

There are, of course, other avenues for dialogue and exchange. Premarital therapeutic sessions are excellent if you can afford them; that also assumes you know you need them. The "I-Can-Handle-It-Syndrome" takes many a delusional form and frequently blinds many of us to our own need for help, or at least advice. There are also stepparenting support groups and survival courses which are available (see Appendix B). But many individuals who consider remarriage with children may not have the time or money for pre-nuptial counseling and support groups. Many people, like myself, go into remarriage without much knowledge as to what is in store. Yet unexpected feelings can be triggered, and if you do not know this may happen or how to get the difficult ones out, you will be in for tough times. You may get ill as I did; your marriage can erode and die; or you may live in a state of just wanting to get by which is a grim approach to life at best.

As mentioned, I wish I had taken more time to learn about the possible impact of the different myths, stepfamily emotions, and relational dynamics, especially when former partners are still angry and hurt at one another. If you can do this, the problems may still be there, but hopefully they will not be as shocking or unexpected. Proactive counseling, dialogue, and other forms of therapy can prepare us, at least in part, for the vicissitudes of stepfamily living. It is not advisable to wait and hope that everything will eventually be all right. One stepmother in full-time therapy declares:

> My husband really had to uncover and examine a world of things about his feelings, guilts, and love for his sons before he was free to experience our child. I had to understand a lot and to accept a lot about what being a parent means to him. . . . We didn't talk nearly enough before we got married. We should have gotten help much earlier. . . .[2]

Unfortunately, most of us seek counseling after the fact when we are in a state of turmoil and chaos, alternating between the disillusionment and crisis phases of stepfamily life. Or we are forced into it by the conciliation courts and family arbitration around custody suits. Yet knowing in advance that this is an expected response to the stress of this kind of family life can be of great help. Knowing that it is the situation itself and not something inherently bad or wrong with us is a freeing and relieving experience. As one stepparent declares,

> My husband and I never discussed how difficult I found being a stepmother. . . . It could have been so much easier if we had talked. The one thing I would tell somebody marrying a divorced man with kids today is to start talking about what is going on with the children and how you feel about it at once. . . .[3]

Another comment:

> Five years into our marriage Walter and I had made all the classic mistakes about stepparenting. Neither of us had explored past feelings and relationships before we married. We did not understand that we were a different kind of family unit and pretended to be like the families we had left . . . none of us dealt with the feelings that gnawed at us, denying their existence until these emotions became our enemies.[4]

If you would like to avoid these stepfamily pitfalls, remember:

Stepparenting Without Guilt Rule #21

Relationships can be difficult and challenging; problems are problems. There are no easy blueprints for happiness in family life, step or otherwise. But talking and listening, being truthful and fair do help.

FOCUS ON THE COUPLE

Based upon my own experience, it is easy to see how children can dominate the remarriage because their needs are the most readily apparent. My husband and I learned the hard way that our marriage and couplehood had to come first. This not only was for survival's sake but recognizes the fact that the quality of the relationship between husband and wife influences the relationship between parent and child, stepparent and stepchild. There is both personal and pragmatic value in keeping the focus on the marriage. As difficult as it may be, it is vital for the couple to come first. Children need to learn and see this because it represents valuable modeling for them in their own future relationships.

Another positive by-product of a strong bonding between husband and wife is increased stepfamily cohesion. The reality of stepfamily life is that the children's needs will often be put before the couple's unless they are firm in their belief that their marriage must assume priority. Sometimes this can take quite a while to achieve. Dealing with all the stepfamily chaos—schedules, visitations, where'd-you leave-your-shoes?—along with unrealistic expectations of bonding with children can create problems between the couple which run so deep that the necessary bonding between the two adults never takes place. All too often the remarriage crashes and burns because there is no strong marital anchor with which to withstand all the stress. Divorce rates offer sad testimony to the fact that many remarriages collapse under the pressure of the children and all the logistics involved.[5] Then everyone loses, especially the children who benefit in the long run if the coupleship is strong. Remarriage can work, but you have to be patient and committed to hard work. Keep this in mind.

Stepparenting Without Guilt Rule #22

A successful second marriage can help children get over the pain of a previous divorce. Mistakes can be openly acknowledged and talked about and the opportunity arises for modeling honesty and sharing knowledge that are earned from experience.

The importance of the couple honoring their partnership cannot be stressed enough since the opportunity for destructive triangles and manipulative behavior are increased in stepfamily situations.[6] Unhealthy triangles can emerge when boundaries are vague or non-existent; for example, mother and children against new stepfather; father and children against new stepmother; daughter against stepmother; son against stepfather; or new couple against ex-spouse and vice versa. There is no etiquette book or standardized rules of behavior on how to deal with all this. Yet the importance of confronting triangles which form in stepfamilies is critical because they generally only serve to reinforce an atmosphere of hostility and silent warfare. Also, firm, clear limits between all concerned minimizes the opportunity for children to play one parent and household off against the other. Talking about this beforehand is a good way to start new step relationships; direct, two-way communication is a key in this process.

If the couple is united and deeply committed from the onset and anticipates that remarried families by their very nature may experience more guilt, resentment, and other problems than intact families, there is a chance to work through the turbulent period of adjustment. It means addressing conflicts which most of us would rather not have to deal with, but that is part of the emotional journey of this way of life. If you cannot learn how to do this, the following is what might happen to you:

> I had Joe's three children every other weekend and every summer for three years before I realized I couldn't take it. Then I continued to have them for three more years before I got the courage to say I didn't want to have them any more. Now I'm so bitter over all the things I hated and had to do that I don't think I can ever get over it. . . . It took me years to move from trying so hard to indifference to anger. If I could do it over, I'd fight back sooner instead of waiting until it's too late to remove the resentments for everything we've done and everything we've lost. I'd ask more of Joe for my own children, and I'd give less of myself to his. . . . Then maybe the two of us could have had more time together.[7]

The good news is that stepfamilies can offer the opportunity of watching a second marriage work which may lessen the sense of failure and defeat from the first. It may even strengthen a positive attitude toward marriage itself. That is not to say it is easy getting there; none of us chooses pain and difficulty willingly. Like going to the dentist, it may be necessary, yet many of us would rather do *anything* but. With more humor and conscious light-heartedness, hopefully we can learn how to cope in constructive rather than destructive ways with the many issues of stepfamily life.

MARRIAGE WORK VS. PARENTING WORK

In conjunction with focusing on the couple, it is important to make a clear distinction between what is marriage work and what is the work of being a parent. Too often in remarriage with children these two areas get confused and this can cause problems later on. Among other things, marriage work includes:

- truthfulness and dependability between the two partners
- sharing labor
- ego support and sympathy
- talking and listening
- sexual satisfaction and the desire to please
- giving more than receiving[8]

Parenting work, on the other hand, requires a different set of activities:

- maintenance of food, shelter, and clothing for children
- guidance and socialization
- discipline
- assistance (both advice and financial help)
- love and respect
- training young people to be independent, then letting go[9]

All the differences between stepfamily members require a great deal of tolerance and mutual forbearance—qualities which our society with its me-first, loner individualism does not encourage. Our whole culture in ways that are both subtle and blatant fosters the expectation of instant results; we are not trained to be patient or to engage in appropriate interdependence. When things do not go as we assumed they would, or the way we want them to (another variation on the theme of needing to be in control), we throw things away, including relationships, which might be salvageable if we choose to work on them. This holds especially true for stepfamily life.

KEYS TO COMMUNICATION

The constant refining of communication, asking questions about feelings and situations is the essence of all healing work. Dialogue forms a bonding, a sense of belonging and relationship, which become the true building blocks of community. The word "community" literally meaning to be in communion with. I know in my own case our stepfamily had to learn how to talk and listen in new and different ways, especially communicating negative feelings. This can be hard for many of us even in the best of circumstances. Not only may we be shy about expressing our feelings (assuming we are even conscious of them), but stepfamily life interrupts our communication process in other ways. Talking about feelings frequently gets delayed or put on hold until the next visitation because there always seems to be some sort of reshuffling due to leave-takings, time rearrangements, dealing with the schedule, and carpooling back and forth. But this reality of stepfamily life can also be used as a way of avoiding dialogue and sweeping conflict aside.

If problems are ignored, they tend to grow. In my own case, I was very good at this, rationalizing that things weren't really all *that* bad, when in fact they were much worse than I allowed myself to feel. All this means engaging in even more emotional sharing. (See Appendix C for some suggestions.) Communication is a must, and while frequently heated, it is *never* boring. Some of our Family Councils have been quite animated. Being able to give voice to terrible thoughts and feelings and *still* be loved. What a concept! It truly is revolutionary for those of us who have not had that experience before in our lives because stepfamily and family life means learning how to *not* avoid heated emotional issues but facing them head-on.

When we keep our feelings buried and allow our mistakes to accumulate, stress levels only build. The success or failure of a stepfamily often depends upon our ability to develop lasting bonds, and one of the ways of achieving this is through talking and especially listening. Communication and non-judgmental listening are among the best ways of showing respect, of honoring another human being; without these vital ingredients, there can be no real relationships or dialogue.

Communication skills and working on issues of self-worth and self-esteem are also key factors in building stepfamily cohesiveness. As stated previously, self-esteem in particular may be low for individuals coming from divorce and disrupted relationships, and this can impede the communication and bonding process of the new stepfamily. Frequently this is due to the fact that the individuals involved often are afraid to express their feelings for fear of being hurt again.

It has been my experience that there is greater reluctance to communicate negative feelings in second marriages because of our desire to succeed. Yet if left unexpressed feelings of shame, failure, and resentment can remain like ghosts haunting stepfamily life. As a culture we do not know how to talk about our feelings or even feel our feelings in coherent, congruent, and meaningful ways. We have so many messages coming from outside sources, the media in general and television in particular, which bombard us constantly with what to think, what to need, what to want, and how to feel that we do not develop these heart muscles for ourselves in our own time, in our own way. As one stepparent comments,

> Struggling to be ourselves in an honest relationship with those we live with and love is surely better than the hidden violence and misery of living by role expectation.[10]

Living by role expectation is an ever-ready trap in many stepfamily situations, especially because of all the myths and stereotypes involved. Talking and sharing in Council is one vehicle whereby we can move toward more honest feelings and goals. Outside assistance in the form of counseling, stepparenting groups, and therapy can be invaluable, but the most important thing is to keep dialogue open and ongoing in the home.

Stepparenting Without Guilt Rule #23

Being a mind-reader in stepfamilies has its drawbacks. Do not assume anything. Talk, and if that does not work, take a break and talk some more. With time and practice, more fulfilling relationships can be negotiated in stepfamily life.

CHAPTER SEVEN

Relationship Saving Suggestions: How It All Can Work

As I CONTINUE TO WORK with adults and children, I often ask myself the question: "What is love?" I believe finally this is what most of us ultimately are seeking within ourselves and with each other, in counseling or not. Yet I am not sure many of us understand what this delicate and demanding emotion entails a great deal of the time. I certainly continue to ponder its meaning in the world and in my work with people, young and old. I have discovered through trial and error, especially in my stepfamily experience, that implementing the words love, compassion, and patience on a daily basis are infinitely harder and more complex than most people imagine.

Is love a feeling or an action? A noun or a verb? A choice or a belief? A father's love vs. a mother's? A stepmother's vs. a biological one's? How do you love a person? How do you generate love in a family and stepfamiliy? T.S. Eliot writes that the major cause of anxiety and depression in this century is our inability to love and be loved.[1] And while it may not be a requirement that you love in order to experience workable relationships, it *does* help. Learning how to love, especially in stepfamily life, is a reality more and more of us are facing these days. Again I ask: How do we go about it? How do we create *that* choice?

THE SUMMUM BONUM

In one of my many forays into second hand bookshops, I came across a small volume by Henry Drummond entitled *The Greatest Thing in the World.*[2] Drummond was a 19th century Scottish evangelist for whom the greatest thing, the *summum bonum*, was (is) love, a love that is waiting to find a pathway to all our hearts.

Drawing upon the popular verse in Chapter 13 of First Corinthians (which ironically was the verse Peter and I had read at our wedding ceremony while four year old Nikki looked on) is well known. Faith, hope, and love, but the greatest of these, the *summum bonum*, the noblest, most supreme gift is love. It is the Prime Mover making all else possible, not only possible but worthwhile.

Drummond provides a point-by-point analysis of this supreme good, breaking down love into nine key areas: patience, kindness, generosity, humility, courtesy, unselfishness, good temper, guilelessness (taking no account of evil), and sincerity. These nine qualities are all in relation to life as we live it daily, for the *summum bonum* of love is a pathway to follow in the secular world. It most definitely is *not* a cloistered virtue. The reason I mention Drummond's work here is that I believe it has many fruitful applications to stepfamily and family life and can be looked upon in counterpoint (and as a possible antidote) to some of the emotional minefields covered in Chapter Five.

Drummond defines patience as love waiting to begin. It is not in a hurry but calm and ready to do its quiet work when the call comes (even from stepchildren and ex-sleeping partners). Since love is understanding it can afford to wait. Kindness is love in action, bringing love into the world and making it manifest. The greatest thing we can do to demonstrate love is to be kind to one another, and most of all we need to lend kindness where it is most difficult (i.e. to the myriad challenges of stepfamily life).

Generosity is Drummond's next quality. It is not a giving of things but an opening of the heart in ways that reject envy and uncharitable feelings of self-centeredness. It is the grace of magnanimity coming through us into the world. What is the point of mimicking the motions—sacrifice, charity, good deeds, playing what we think are the right or required roles—if there is no heart in them? For this is all about heart and finding that quiet place where our hearts touch and meet.

Next comes humility. For Drummond, being humble is the force of love disavowing its own self-satisfaction but working quietly and silently for someone or something else. Humility does not want any recognition other than to be itself. Drummond likens humility to love in hiding, poised to work in the world without recognition or accolade. Stepparenting in particular offers ample opportunity for this kind of act, for it involves a type of giving that often comes without visible rewards.

Related to this is courtesy: love manifesting in social relationships and finding politeness in little things. In the very deepest sense a gentleman or a gentlewoman is one who moves gently in the world with love. It requires no translation but rather possesses its own quiet eloquence. One's character becomes the message, not the words themselves. (As Drummond says: We can all feel the beat of love inside a kind heart, even if the words of that heart are unintelligible or never even uttered.)

Next comes unselfishness. This means that we eliminate the personal, by giving ourselves to something that is truly difficult (a.k.a. parenting and stepparenting). Drummond writes that the only greatness of any value is that of unselfish love. It is important not to confuse the unselfishness Drummond refers to with self-denial. Self-denial, according to him, is a grave mistake and very misguided, a trap many of us fall into, especially in stepfamily interactions. Only self-denial which has unselfishness at its root is of lasting worth.

As Corinthians says "Love is not provoked," and for Drummond good temper is the bedrock of love. He is particularly relentless in his pursuit of ill temper and devotes more time and energy to it in his small book than any of the other categories. He calls bad temper one of the most destructive elements in human nature and writes, "The peculiarity of ill temper is that it is the vice of the virtuous." It is the unloving character for those of us stepparents especially who profess to be hard-working, patient, and dutiful while harboring anger, resentment, and larceny in our hearts.

Guilelessness, which is the grace of unsuspicious and unpretentious people, comes next. Suspicion only shrivels us up; whereas faith and belief—being without guile—open us like a flower. To think no evil is not stupidity or slowness but a choice, an action in the world. To respect another is the first step in the restoration of one's own self-respect. In other words, my positive ideal of Nikki acts upon her as a pattern and pathway of hope for what she may yet be and become. I remind myself that the opposite is also true: Nikki's love and trust for me allow me to flower and blossom in unique and unexpected ways as well. In this way we contribute in an ever-widening manner to the lives of those around us.

Sincerity is last. It means celebrating truth, whatever that truth may be and wherever it is found. An individual who loves, loves the truth no less or more than people. Sincerity means searching for what is *real;* it requires looking for the truth with a humble and open mind, as painful at times as that may be. Sincerity is the self-restraint which refuses to capitalize on another's faults; it is a charity of heart that does not expose weakness but sees things as they are and is gladdened to find them better than suspicion or fear. Once again, stepfamily life offers many opportunities for this kind of sincerity and honest humility.

These nine qualities put together comprise the *summum bonum*: love.

Drummond's final defense of love as the supreme thing is that it lasts. It is the one thing that lasts, always. Counselors and therapists can help reveal angry thoughts and difficult feelings, and it certainly is important to address these issues, but love becomes the true alchemical and transforming element. Family and stepfamily life offer an education in learning how to live with love. They represents our work in the world involving patience, generosity, kindness, humility, unselfishness, guilelessness, courtesy, sincerity, and good humor. Without these qualities as a centering agent, productive, healthy relationships are difficult to achieve or maintain. So remember:

Stepparenting Without Guilt Rule #24

Honesty, humility, humor, and respect: these are the bedrock of stepfamily life. From here you and your family members, if you choose to do so, can move toward love.

BEYOND WAR WITHIN THE SELF

Recently I came across this statement from Mahatma Gandhi in one of my many notebooks which I think has applications to stepfamily life:

> Experience has taught me that civility is the most difficult part of Satyagraha [Gandhi's philosophy]. Civility does not here mean the mere outward gentleness of speech cultivated for the occasion but an inborn gentleness and desire to do the opponent good.

A genuine and sincere generosity of spirit to do one's opponent good. This is something well worth thinking about in relationship to stepfamilies, especially since it is so easy for us to pose our stepchildren and the "ex" (or current spouse and children) as "the enemy." How important it is to not polarize between me and you, us and them, new family and old but learning to perceive the "other" as a reflection of one's own self, a reflection of all creation in fact. It is that exquisite and sacred moment where the membrane of difference sloughs off and we feel connected at the very core. Healing through relationship is a mysterious process, but the pathway is clear: it is learning how to love one person through time, quietly, privately, alone; that is what heals. Our personal and collective healing as individuals and families are all tied together, inextricably bound in a web of interconnectedness. I personally believe the crucible of family and stepfamily life is where the real education of the world both begins and ends. It means being there for what is and allowing the depths to surface, painful as they may be, pressing out what is inside so that it can connect with others, not expressionless but expression-filled.

The Talmud says that God wants the heart, and true healing and integration mean learning how to share that part of our being, one to another, finding a pathway to both personal and collective community. As Stephen Levine, a well-known healer, comments:

> . . . we must not only acknowledge but move to embrace that part of ourselves which has been blocked off and ignored. Healing requires looking directly at the rawness of our pain.

> In many instances, this means that we relearn what we have been taught about pain; that is, to escape or run and hide from it. We must start to relate to pain in a different way if we are to heal, learning how to reach and embrace the compassion in our hearts. . . . Not at all an easy task when so many of us have learned to defend against pain with denial, judgment, repressed anger, or voiced sarcasm.[3]

Stepfamily and family life offer ample opportunities for this healing journey by presenting so many challenges to personal honesty and emotional integrity. The word "heal" means to be or to become whole again. And talking about wholeness means talking about relationships, both with one's self and with others; talking about relationships means working with them, putting things together again, moving through the hurt and misunderstanding which are inherent to them. As I said earlier: the way out is by going in and through. And it helps to remind ourselves as we move through the many vicissitudes of stepfamily life that there are exercises in healing which we can engage in on a daily basis. A few of my own include the following reminders:

- Peace in the world starts first with peace in my own heart.
- Concentrate on the meaning of forgiveness. Forgiveness never ends
- Consider the underlying motives of the heart with compassion.
- Practice brings forth the fruit of patience.
- Patience keeps me in touch with inner peacefulness and serenity.[4]

I remind myself never to forget the healing power of forgiveness, forgiveness of others, and forgiveness of my own self and human frailties. The peace-giving power of forgiveness heals all if we only let it. And patience is a commodity essential in all walks of life. Stepfamily life offers many opportunities for rising above the heat and anger of the moment and choosing a different kind of response. I remind myself also of another truth: one cannot love to order; one only grows in love daily, bit by patient bit. Only then can love generate love. It is a process of induction, the creation of a new heart, broken down then reconstructed and reconfigured into something new. You learn that love is not only a feeling but also a choice, perhaps the most important one there is.

There is also the sense from being in a stepfamily of the kind of giving Albert Schweitzer writes about: a fundamental respect for life, with or without the biological connection. For on some level—emotional, spiritual, cosmic, mysterious—we are all connected. Being in a stepfamily invites us to learn a greater flexibility because there are more opportunities to compare differences and learn about life. Being judgmental must go, and this makes stepfamilies a crucible where true tolerance can begin. There can be a deeper substance to your life if you are willing to try.

From a more pragmatic standpoint, the odds are growing against being a mate and parent in the traditional context because by the millennium stepparents and stepparenting will form the majority of family life in this country.[5] As old structures break down, we are being called upon to learn, whether we like it or not, new ways of being with one another, of communicating with one another. Somehow stepfamily life parallels this development, this evolution in patience and tolerance—a paradigm for our entire planet, perhaps. Which brings me to the most important point of all:

Stepparenting Without Guilt Rule #25

The greatest gift you can give your stepchild (or child) is permission to be happy in both homes. We do not all have to act or think the same way, and learning how to honor differences is vital in all aspects of life.

Over and above what I hope have been useful and practical tools for improving familial interactions, in the final analysis stepfamily and family life open up the opportunity for spiritual deepening. This is especially true when confronting so many difficult emotions with stark honesty and trying to work through them in a spirit of non-violence and good-will. Family life itself becomes a spiritual path and while many may not agree with this assessment, it has been my personal and professional experience that this potential is there. While the journey of stepfamily life may be challenging, the rewards of reaching satisfying relationships are infinitely worthwhile. You need to hang in there to help grow decent human beings of the stepfamily kind.

Epilogue

As THIS BOOK WENT TO PUBLICATION, my stepdaughter's biological mother passed away from metastasized cancer. I would like to acknowledge her in memoriam.

Virginia Curry Kreis
March 12, 1939 – October 4, 1999

APPENDIX A

Rules in Brief

Rule #1

You cannot take away the pain of the past or pretend it's not real. Recognize and accept stepfamily problems for what they are and know that in most stepfamilies the best way to achieve genuine bonding is to work through the hard times.

Rule #2

A future stepparent needs to assess the many stepfamily variables before entering into an agreement. Do not abdicate personal responsibility to educate yourself about the ins and outs of stepfamily life. This does not necessarily mean you will decide against remarriage, but at least you will have a clearer picture of what you are getting yourself into.

Rule #3

Be prepared from the beginning that stepfamilies do not function the same as intact, nuclear families. If you expect them to do so, you may experience even more trouble. Stepfamilies are their own separate reality and require a different way of life.

Rule #4

Good relationships can exist without love. They do, however, require consistency and trust. If at first you are unable to experience equity of feeling with your stepchildren, at least concentrate on equity of treatment. Fairness goes a long way toward earning respect.

Rule #5

Beware of stepparent dogooderism. You cannot change the past, and you may make things harder for yourself by trying to "make things better" or "set things right." Sometimes being a good stepparent requires knowing the virtue of restraint.

Rule #6

Question the natural parent when he or she promises "to take care of everything." No matter how sincere and well intentioned your future spouse may be, practically speaking it may not work out that way in day-to-day reality. In stepfamily life some healthy skepticism may be necessary for self-preservation.

Rule #7

The growth of personal responsibility is in inverse proportion to excessive pampering. Giving too much to your stepchild only impedes his or her acquisition of this important adaptive tool. Sometimes less ends up being more because it is important for children to be held accountable for their own behavior.

Rule #8

Stepparenting (and biological parenting) are not about winning a popularity contest. They're about doing the job that is called for, and sometimes that job is tough. Be clear when, where, and on what issues you intend to take a stand.

Rule #9

Restraint and patience are important in most instances requiring discipline, but do not hesitate to take appropriate action with your stepchild when called for. Remember that a failure to act can be just as damaging as being overly strict.

Rule #10

Know the virtue (and necessity) of accepting what you cannot change and work from there. Do not try to fix everything all at once, especially with stepsiblings. Genuine positive regard and love cannot be achieved overnight where children of remarriage are concerned.

Rule #11

First form firm boundaries followed by consistency, appropriate concern, and respect. These are important in any family but absolutely essential in stepfamilies and may help in warding off another divorce.

Rule #12

Taking a stand as a stepparent is especially important around custody and visitation settlements because you will have to deal on a daily basis with the decision of the courts. This is not being mean but realistic, and it is important to be aware of this fact.

Rule #13

Playing the "Who's-to-Blame?" Game is a no-win situation for all concerned. It only serves to fuel further antagonism between stepfamily members rather than mutuality and compromise. It is not a question of who is to blame but how you and your stepfamily go about accepting personal responsibility.

Rule #14

Your stepfamily situation may generate a great deal of emotional reactivity and frequently volatile feelings are there because stepfamily members hurt in a lot of places. Often it is both useful and important to take a deep breath and count to ten before responding.

Rule #15

Avoid "should, would, could." Unless you are honest and straightforward, especially with your feelings, you won't get far in stepfamily (and family) life. Feelings are not good or bad; they simply are and need to be respected. Once they are shared honestly, the behaviors which accompany them can be worked on.

Rule #16

If you honestly and sincerely cannot deal with your stepchild, do not lie to yourself that you can. Accept your limitations and don't punish yourself for something you are unable to achieve. Honor what you can do and work from there.

Rule #17

There is a point where your biological children come first, and this has nothing to do with being mean or wicked. You do not have to save your stepchildren at the expense of your own off-spring. Being firm and realistic about their needs will help you be a better stepparent as well.

Rule #18

Happiness and trust cannot be achieved when fear and anxiety are at their base. This applies to all members of the stepfamily, adult and child alike. Learning how to view fear and anxiety as signposts which can direct us toward new and positive ways of interacting is important in stepfamily life.

Rule #19

Do not talk ill of the absent parent or other stepfamily members. Mean-spirited comments only come back to haunt you and reinforce the evil stepparent myth. While it is important to acknowledge anger, you also have a choice how to express it; sometimes prudent detachment is the best policy.

Rule #20

Stepfamilies are born of loss. Accept and honor this fact and the heartache which accompanies it. With work and persistence, belief in the new stepfamily can arise.

Rule #21

Relationships can be difficult and challenging; problems are problems. There are no easy blueprints for happiness in family life, step or otherwise. But talking and listening, being truthful and fair do help.

Rule #22

A successful second marriage can help children get over the pain of a previous divorce. Mistakes can be openly acknowledged and talked about and the opportunity arises for modeling honesty and sharing knowledge that are earned from experience.

Rule #23

Being a mind-reader in stepfamilies has its drawbacks. Do not assume anything. Talk, and if that does not work, take a break and talk some more. With time and practice, more fulfilling relationships can be negotiated in stepfamily life.

Rule #24

Honesty, humility, humor, and respect: these are the bedrock of stepfamily life. From here you and your family members, if you choose to do so, can move toward love.

Rule #25

The greatest gift you can give your stepchild (or child) is permission to be happy in both homes. We do not all have to act or think the same way, and learning how to honor differences is vital in all aspects of life.

APPENDIX B

Addresses You Should Know

The Center for Families in Transition
(c/o Dr. Judith Wallerstein)
P.O. Box 157
Corte Madera, CA 94976
Phone (415) 924-5750
FAX (415) 388-1225

The Children of Separation and Divorce Center, Inc.
2000 Century Plaza, Suite 121
Columbia, MD 21044
Phone (410) 740-9553
FAX (301) 596-1677
http://cosd.bayside.net
E-mail cos2@juno.com

Parents Without Partners
401 No. Michigan Avenue
Chicago, IL 60611
International main number (312) 644-6610
FAX for International Office (312) 321-5194
http://www.parentswithoutpartners.org

Planned Parenthood Federation of America, Inc.
810 Seventh Avenue
New York, New York 10019
Phone (800) 669-0156
http://www.plannedparenthood.org/MAIN.HTM

The Stepfamily Association of America, Inc.
650 J Street, Suite 205
Lincoln, NE 68508
Phone (800) 735-0329
FAX (402) 477-8317
http://www.stepfamily.org
E-mail stepfamfs@aol.com

Step Family Foundation, Inc.
333 West End Avenue
New York, New York 10023
Phone (212) 877-3244
FAX (212) 362-7030
http://www.stepfamily.org
E-mail staff@stepfamily.org

The Stepfamily Network, Inc.
2600 Central Avenue, Suite L
Union City, CA 94587
Phone (800) 487-1073
http://www.stepfamily.net/index.shtml

The Stepparenting Connection (TSC)
1000 Peacetree Industrial Blvd., Suite 6
Suwanee, GA 30024
Phone (770) 945-2469
http://www.tsconnection.org

You can also check your local Yellow Pages for counseling and therapy services.

APPENDIX C

Convenient Checklist of Topics for Discussion

1. Set up one-on-one time with your stepchild before the marriage so you can get some sense of what it will be like later on.
2. Ask yourself sincerely whether you are willing to put in the time and patience for a genuine relationship to emerge.
3. Explore feelings of isolation and powerlessness.
4. Learn to be as honest as possible about your feelings without being mean-spirited or malicious.
5. Keep track of what works for you and what does not.
6. Develop new stepfamily traditions of your own.
7. Find ways to counteract both physical and emotional stress.
8. If possible, provide each stepfamily member with his or her own space to lessen feelings of territoriality and being invaded.
9. Keep a positive but realistic attitude.

10 Focus on creating a strong bond between the couple.
11 Learn how to take responsibility for your own actions, not everybody else's.
12 Examine and discuss the impact of various stepfamily myths.
13 Deal with the practical logistics of the schedule and visitation on an ongoing basis.
14 Talk about the different needs and values between the various households involved.
15 Examine the negative emotions and competition for love and affection between stepfamily members.
16 Mourn the loss of the first family if this hasn't been done or again if necessary.
17 Deal with the relationship between in-laws and ex-in-laws.
18 Discuss how to manage stepsibling and half-sibling rivalry as well as watching for the possibility of increased sexuality in stepfamilies.
19 Talk about who is responsible for discipline.
20 Investigate and discuss financial issues that are unique to your stepfamily life.

Notes

Chapter One

1 Jerry Adler, "How Children Mourn," *Newsweek*, September 22, 1997, p. 58. Also see the pioneering work of Dr. Judith Wallerstein from the Center for Families in Transition on the impact of divorce on children.

2 Cherie Burns, *Stepmotherhood: How to Survive Without Feeling Frustrated, Left Out, or Wicked*, Time Books, Random House Inc., New York, 1985, p. xv introduction.

3 Elizabeth Einstein, *The StepFamily: Living, Loving, and Learning*, MacMillan Publishing Co., New York, 1982, pp. 8-9.

4 Linda Craven, *Stepfamilies: New Patterns of Harmony*, Julian Messner, New York, 1982, p. 48.

5 Nan Bauer Maglin and Nancy Schniedewind, *Women and Stepfamilies: Voices of Anger and Love*, Temple University Press, Philadelphia, 1989, p. 13.

6 Dan Kaercher, "Making Stepchildren Part of the Family," *Better Homes and Gardens*, Vol 63, No. 2, February, 1985, p. 67 and Vicki Jarmulowski, "The Blended Family: Who Are They?" *Ms. Magazine*, February, 1985, p. 34.

7 Emily B. & John S. Visher, *Stepfamilies: A Guide to Working With Stepparents and Stepchildren*, Brunner/Mazel Publishers, New York, 1979, p. 36.

8 Lucile Duberman, *The Reconstituted Family: A Study of Remarried Couples and Their Children*, Nelson-Hall Publishers, Chicago, 1975, pp. 2-3.

9 Same as above, p. 124.
10 Elsa Ferri, *Stepchildren: A National Study*, A Report From the National Child Development Study, Nelson Publishing Co., London, 1984, p. 1.
11 Barbara Kantrowitz and Pat Wright, "Step by Step: The 21st Century Family," *Newsweek*, Special Edition Winter/Spring, 1990, p. 27 and Ferri, *Stepchildren: A National Study*, pp. 76-77.
12 Kantrowitz & Wright, *Newsweek*, p. 27.
13 Visher & Visher, *Stepfamilies*, pp. 16-17, and Ferri, *Stepchildren: A National Study*, p. 7.
14 Ferri, *Stepchildren: A National Study*, p. 7.
15 Elizabeth Einstein, "Five Myths About Stepfamilies," *Parents*, Vol. 58, No. 11, November, 1983, pp. 90, 92 and Einstein, *The StepFamily*, p. 44.
16 Visher & Visher, *Stepfamilies*, pp. 54, 209.
17 Ferri, *Stepchildren: A National Study*, p. 76.
18 Einstein, *The StepFamily*, p. 170.

Chapter Two

1 Craven, *Stepfamilies*, pp.52-53.
2 Burns, *Stepmotherhood*, p. 75.
3 Craven, *Stepfamilies*, pp. 55-56 and Ruther Roosevelt and Jeannette Lofas, *Living in Step*, Stein and Day Publishers, New York, 1976, p. 143.
4 Visher & Visher, *Stepfamilies*, p. 139.
5 Burns, *Stepmotherhood*, p. 100.
6 Same as above.
7 Same as above, p. 35.
8 Candace Perry Ribnick, "Living Happily Ever After in a Stepfamily," *New Orleans*, August, 1982, p. 44.
9 Visher & Visher, *Stepfamilies*, pp. 220-221.
10 Burns, *Stepmotherhood*, p. 173.
11 James D. Eckler, *Step-by-Stepparenting: A Guide to Successful Living With a Blended Family*, Betterway Publications, Inc., Virginia, 1988, p. 67.
12 Maglin & Schniedewind, *Women and Stepfamilies*, p. 206.
13 Duberman, *The Reconstituted Family*, p. 117.
14 Eckler, *Step-by-Stepparenting*, p. 125.
15 Craven, *Stepfamilies*, p. 109.

Chapter Three

1 Visher & Visher, *Stepfamilies*, p. 81 and Craven, *Stepfamilies*, pp. 175-176.
2 Maglin & Schniedewind, *Women and Stepfamilies*, p. 97.
3 Isoline Ricci, *Mom's House, Dad's House: Making Shared Custody Work*, MacMillan Publishing Co., New York, 1980, p. 43 and Einstein, "Five Myths About Stepfamilies," *Parents*, p. 90.
4 Martha Ward Dudley, "Bad Mousie," *The Tall Book of Make-Believe*, Harper & Row Publishers, New York, 1950, pp.41-47.
5 Meredith Kay, "I Married My Husband's Kids," *Parents*, Vol. 58, No. 11, November, 1983, p. 86-87 and Visher & Visher, *Stepfamilies*, pp. 174-175.
6 Ferri, *Stepchildren: A National Study*, p. 116; also see the work of Dr. Judith Wallerstein.
7 Craven, *Stepfamilies*, pp. 17-19.
8 Visher & Visher, *Stepfamilies*, p. 175.
9 Ferri, *Stepchildren: A National Study*, p. 119.
10 Maglin & Schniedewind, *Women and Stepfamilies*, p. 199.
11 Einstein, *The StepFamily*, p. 161ff.
12 Maglin & Schniedewind, *Women and Stepfamilies*, p. 22
13 Burns, *Stepmotherhood*, p. 3
14 Maglin & Schniedewind, *Women and Stepfamilies*, p. 311 and Einstein, *The Stepfamily*, p. 144.
15 Einstein, *The StepFamily*, p. 84.
16 Duberman, *The Reconstituted Family*, p. 84.
17 Ricci, *Mom's House, Dad's House*, p. 16.
18 Visher & Visher, *Stepfamilies*, p. 135.
19 Same as above, pp. 134-135.

Chapter Four

1 Burns, *Stepmotherhood*, p. vx introduction, p. 5.
2 Save as above, p.3
3 From *The Half Parent* by Brenda Maddox, 1975 cited in Visher & Visher, *Stepfamilies*, p. 56.
4 Einstein, *The StepFamily*, p. 108.
5 Maglin & Schniedewind, *Women and Stepfamilies*, pp. 149-150.
6 Visher & Visher, *Stepfamilies*, p. 50.
7 Einstein, *The StepFamily*, p. 108.
8 Duberman, *The Reconstituted Family*, p. 100.

9 See Maglin & Schniedewind, *Women and Stepfamilies: Voices of Anger and Love* as entire book deals with theme of ambivalence and conflicting stepmother emotions.
10 Visher & Visher, *Stepfamilies*, p. 52.
11 Eckler, *Step-by-Stepparenting*, p. 89.
12 Einstein, *The StepFamily*, p. 101.
13 Ferri, *Stepchildren: A National Study*, p. 117.
14 Maglin & Schniedewind, *Women and Stepfamilies*, p. xi introduction.
15 Same as above, p. xii introduction.
16 Einstein, *The StepFamily*, p. 118.

Chapter Five

1 Visher & Visher, *Stepfamilies*, p. 44.
2 Same as above, p. 35.
3 Einstein, *The StepFamily*, pp. 108-109.
4 Roosevelt & Lofas, *Living in Step*, p. 33.
5 Same as above, p. 116.
6 Jarmulowski, "The Blended Family: Who Are They?" *Ms. Magazine*, see pp. 39-40.
7 Roosevelt & Lofas, *Living in Step*, p. 34.
8 Einstein, *The StepFamily*, pp. 121
9 Same as above.
10 Visher & Visher, *Stepfamilies*, p. 65.
11 Burns, *Stepmotherhood*, pp. 8, 22.
12 Visher & Visher, *Stepfamilies*, p. 99.
13 Same as above, p. 216.
14 Duberman, *The Reconstituted Family*, p. 80.
15 Visher & Visher, *Stepfamilies*, p. 30.
16 Same as above, p. 240.
17 Roosevelt & Lofas, *Living in Step*, p. 51.
18 Duberman, *The Reconstituted Family*, p. 53.
19 Same as above, p. 68.
20 Jarmulowski, "The Blended Family: Who Are They?"*Ms. Magazine*, p. 40.
21 Maglin & Schniedewind, *Women and Stepfamilies*, p. xi introduction.
22 Same as above, p. 240.
23 Einstein, *The StepFamily*, p. 167.

24 Maglin & Schniedewind, *Women and Stepfamilies*, pp. 324-325 and Eckler, *Step-by-Stepparenting*, p. 49.
25 Einstein, *The Stepfamily*, p. 7-8.
26 *Diagnostic and Statistical Manual of Mental Disorders*, 4th Edition (DSM-4), American Psychiatric Association, Washington, DC, 1994, pp. 427-429.
27 Craven, *Stepfamilies*, p. 75.
28 Einstein, *The StepFamily*, p. 8.
29 See Elisabeth Kubler-Ross, *On Death and Dying*, 1969.

Chapter Six

1 See the work of Jack Zimmerman and Virginia Coyle, *The Way of Council*, Las Vegas, Nevada, Bramble Books, 1996, for suggestions.
2 Burns, *Stepmotherhood*, pp. 156-157.
3 Same as above, p. 112.
4 Einstein, *The StepFamily*, p. 124.
5 Remarriage divorce rates waver between 40% and 44%. See Ricci, *Mom's House, Dad's House*, p. 45 and Visher & Visher, *Stepfamilies*, p. xix introduction.
6 Einstein, *The Stepfamily*, p.179 and Burns, *Stepmotherhood*, p. 28.
7 Roosevelt & Lofas, *Living in Step*, p. 57.
8 Duberman, *The Reconstituted Family*, p. 102.
9 Same as above, p. 107.
10 Maglin & Schniedewind, *Women and Stepfamilies*, p. 251.

Chapter Seven

1 Cited in Eckler, *Step-by-Stepparenting*, p. 56.
2 Henry Drummond, *The Greatest Thing in the World*, Fleming H. Revell Company, New Jersey, (no date - originally from speech given in England, 1884), p. 60.
3 Ralph Earle, "At the Heart of Healing," *Sun Magazine*, Issue No. 167, October, 1989, p. 5
4 Excerpts condensed and paraphrased from *The Daily Word, Silent Unity,* Unity Village, Missouri, 1988-1989; also see Ken Cloke's work, *Mediation: Revenge and the Magic of Forgiveness*, Santa Monica, California, Center for Dispute Resolution, 1994, for suggestions.
5 Eckler, *Step-by-Stepparenting*, p. 9.

References

Adler, Jerry, "How Children Mourn," *Newsweek*, September 22, 1997.

Burns, Cherie, *Stepmotherhood: How to Survive Without Feeling Frustrated, Left Out, or Wicked*, New York, Time Books, Random House, 1985.

Craven, Linda, *Stepfamilies: New Patterns of Harmony*, New York, Julian Messner, 1982.

Cloke, Kenneth, *Mediation: Revenge and the Magic of Forgiveness*, Santa Monica, California, Center for Dispute Resolution, 1994.

Duberman, Lucile, *The Reconstituted Family: A Study of Remarried Couples and Their Children*, Chicago, Nelson Hall Publishers, 1975.

Earle, Ralph, "At the Heart of Healing," *Sun Magazine*, No. 167, October, 1989.

Eckler, James D., *Step-by-Stepparenting: A Guide to Successful Living with a Blended Family*, Virginia, Betterway Publications, Inc., 1988.

Einstein, Elizabeth, *The Step Family: Living, Loving, and Learning*, New York, MacMillan Publishing Co., 1982.

Einstein, Elizabeth, "Five Myths About Stepfamilies," *Parents*, Vol. 58, No. 11, 1983.

Ephron, Delia, *Funny Sauce: Us, the Ex, the Ex's New Mate, the New Mate's Ex, and the Kids*, New York, Viking Penguin Inc., 1986.

Ferri, Elsa, *Stepchildren: A National Study: A Report from the National Child Development Study,* London, Nelson Publishing Co., 1984.

Jarmulowski, Vicki, "The Blended Family: Who Are They?", *Ms. Magazine,* February, 1985.

Kaercher, Dan, "Making Stepchildren Part of the Family," *Better Homes and Garden,* Vol. 63, No. 2, February, 1985.

Kantowitz, Barbara and Pat Wright, "Step by Step: The 21st Century Family," *Newsweek,* Special Edition, Winter/Spring, 1990.

Kramer, Matt, *Conversations Before a Marriage,* Santa Monica, California, Curly Maple Media, 1997.

Maglin, Nan Bauer and Nancy Schniedewind, *Women and Stepfamilies: Voices of Anger and Love,* Philadelphia, Temple University Press, 1989.

Meredith, Kay, "I Married My Husband's Kids," *Parents,* No. 58, No. 11, November, 1983.

Ribnick, Candace Perry, "Living Happily Ever After in a Stepfamily," *New Orleans,* August, 1984.

Ricci, Isolina, *Mom's House, Dad's House: Making Shared Custody Work,* New York, MacMillan Publishing Co., 1980.

Roberts, Francis, "Stepfamilies: Stresses and Surprises," *Parent,* Vol. 56, No. 3, March, 1981.

Roosevelt, Ruth and Jeannette Lofas, *Living in Step,* New York, Stein and Day Publishers, 1976.

Rosin, Mark Bruce, "Instant Fatherhood: Add Kids and Shake," *Parents,* Vol. 59, No. 10, October, 1984.

Schildkraut, Midge L., "Stepparenting Problems: The Best Ways to Solve Them," *Good Housekeeping,* Vol. 198, No. 1, January, 1984.

Visher, Emily B. and John S. Visher, *Stepfamilies: A Guide to Working with Stepparents and Stepchildren,* New York, Brunner/Mazel Publishers, 1979.

Watrous, Peter, "Step-etiquette," *Psychology Today,* Vol. 18, No. 1, January, 1984.

Zimmerman, Jack and Virginia Coyle, *The Way of Council,* Las Vegas, Nevada, Bramble Books, 1996.

MAURINE DOERKEN is in private practice as a licensed Marriage, Family, and Child Therapist in the state of California. Previously she has worked as an elementary and secondary school teacher both there and in England. Ms. Doerken received her BA in English Literature in 1972 from UCLA where she was nominated as a Departmental Scholar (graduating Magna Cum Laude, Phi Beta Kappa). By 1980 she had earned two teaching credentials and a Masters of Science in Education from USC, and in 1994 a Masters in Clinical Psychology from Antioch University, Los Angeles. Currently she is an active member of CAMFT (California Assn. of Marriage and Family Therapists).

Ms. Doerken's other published work includes *Classroom Combat: Teaching and Television,* excerpts in *Rereading America: The Borzoi College Reader,* and articles and reviews for *Educational Technology Magazine.* She lives in Santa Monica, California with her husband and four children.